"A Vindication Of My Conduct"

The General Court-Martial
of Lieutenant Colonel George Etherington
of the 60th or Royal American Regiment

Held on the Island of St. Lucia
in the West Indies in October 1781
and the

Extraordinary Story Regarding
the Surrender of the Island of St. Vincent's
In the British Caribbean
During the American Revolution

Dr. Todd E. Harburn and Rodger Durham

HERITAGE BOOKS, INC.

Published 2002 by

HERITAGE BOOKS, INC.
1540E Pointer Ridge Place, Bowie, Maryland 20716
1-800-398-7709
www.heritagebooks.com

ISBN 0-7884-2092-5

A Complete Catalog Listing Hundreds of Titles
On History, Genealogy, and Americana
Available Free Upon Request

Acclaim for *"A Vindication of My Conduct"*

"The surrender of the Island of St. Vincent in 1779 was only one skirmish in the global war between France and Britain that grew out of the American Revolution. But the court martial record of Lt. Col. George Etherington, the unfortunate British officer who commanded St. Vincent, has much to say about racial, military, political, and commercial rivalries in the prosperous Caribbean sugar islands, including the efforts of the native Caribs to retain their lands. Todd Harburn and Rodger Durham have done a service by publishing the court martial of Lt. Col. George Etherington and revealing the complicated relationships and the varied cast of characters behind the events that unfolded on St. Vincent."

Brian Leigh Dunnigan, Curator of Maps, William L. Clements Library; Editor of *Pierre Pouchot's Memoirs on the Late War in North America;* Historian/Author of several books concerning the American Revolutionary War eras at Forts Niagara, Michilimackinac and including *Frontier Metropolis; Picturing Early Detroit*

— ✦✦✦✦✦ —

"George Etherington is most widely remembered as the commandant of the important Great Lakes post of Michilimackinac when it was captured by allies of Chief Pontiac in 1763. During the Revolution, (the main focus of this book), he was given military command of the Carribean Island of Saint Vincent. There he clashed violently with the civil governor, Valentine Morris, who tried to make him the scapegoat for the island's capture by the French. Dr. Todd Harburn's intense research (with assistance from Saint Vincent resident Rodger Durham) has uncovered significant new information that largely exonerates Etherington and shows that he was in many respects, a victim of Morris' incompetence and other circumstances beyond his control. The Court Martial Trial of Lieutenant Colonel George Etherington is an interesting and thought provoking look at a unique soldier, the 18th century British military judicial system, and a little known phase of the American Revolution."

Tim J. Todish, author of *America's FIRST First World War: The French and Indian War 1754-1763,* and the editor of *The Annotated and Illustrated Journals of Major Robert Rogers.*

✤ CONTENTS

⚜ LIST OF ILLUSTRATIONS & MAPS

✠ PREFACE

THAT THIS BOOK even came to fruition is somewhat of a surprise since it was never intended to be a book in the first place. Several years of researching the life of a little-known, American-born British officer, one George Etherington, resulted in the first ever in-depth biographical sketch about him. Although not a remarkable officer, he was nonetheless capable, and was described as a "good and loyal" officer. Aside from the fact that he had been the unfortunate commandant at British-held Fort Michilimackinac in present-day upper Michigan during the Indian Uprising of 1763 known as Pontiac's Conspiracy, not much was known about his life and later military career until the aforementioned recent publication. All of this, perhaps, would not have been of particular significance were it not for his later involvement in the surrender of St. Vincent's Island in the British Caribbean during the American Revolution. This event had received only minimal attention in the past, and that being of a more general nature, including some "second-guessing" by some other historians. Shortly following publication of my biographical research on him, the actual trial transcripts of the 1781 court-martial at St. Lucia involving Etherington and his adversary, Governor Valentine Morris, Esq. of St. Vincent's, were located for me, long having been buried in the archive collections of the Public Record Office in Kew, England. To my surprise, albeit delight, upon reviewing these transcripts, it was satisfying to note that the initial personal conclusions I had argued in support of Etherington's cause, after reading what scant information was available, were correct, despite having disagreed with several factions of those previously published general accounts.

It was at this time that I decided to review this most fascinating story further, particularly since the trial transcripts themselves had never before been published. With the kind permission of the Public Record Office, it was decided to conduct a more expanded and in-depth analysis, hence the idea for a full-length book.

While at first glance this topic might seem somewhat narrow and obscure, in reality it is not, for several reasons. The story of the surrender of St. Vincent's Island in the Caribbean corridor during the American Revolution is much more than just a relating of some unknown military trial in a remote portion of the world. It involved an intense personal conflict between Etherington and the colonial governor there during the time, as well as the extensive participation of the native Carib Indians. The story actually developed over a several-year period and culminated in the court-martial. It also entails the conflict indigenous to both the American and Caribbean colonies between colonial government and the British military; a conflict which was responsible in part for British losses in both corridors during the Revolution. Each Caribbean Island has a unique story regarding its involvement in the American Revolution, most of which are not generally known. This is particularly true of St. Vincent's, especially since the previous published histories have "glossed over" this important event. The newly revealed trial transcripts provide answers to many questions, which we have analyzed, annotated, and critiqued in the manuscript. Moreover, with the renewed interest in the Caribbean corridor of the American Revolution among historians and authors in recent years, this new evaluation adds to the continuing expansion of information concerning the various related topics of this era, not in the least of which contains the story of the famous 60th or Royal American Regiment and its involvement in the events at St. Vincent's. The Royal Americans had served with distinction in almost every major engagement during the French and Indian War, and later played important roles in both the West Indies and southern campaigns in the American colonies during the American Revolution.

During the course of my initial research for the aforementioned Etherington biographical sketch, I had been placed in contact with Mr. Rodger Durham, a resident of Bequia Island, in the country of St. Vincent's and The Grenadines. Rodger, a successful businessman/ owner of a plastics company and former U.S. resident (Texas), has lived on Bequia Island for the last fourteen years. "Semi-retired" and currently working at a local yacht club, he has had a serious interest in the history of St. Vincent's, Bequia and the Grenadines. Rodger has been extremely helpful and most generous in sharing his knowledge with me, particularly with regard to the indigenous Carib Indians. At the time of my initial contact with him, he was completing a database history of St. Vincent's/Bequia for local high school students, their parents and tourists. In the ensuing two years, our correspondence as colleagues in history as well as our friendship progressed, and as my idea for the book developed, I eventually asked Rodger if he would accept an offer to be co-author in this endeavor. He was slightly reluctant at first, not sure that he could contribute extensively (as he stated) to what I had in mind or perhaps expected. However, on the contrary, Rodger deserves every credit as co-author, since he has been as equally diligent in providing not only information, but a unique perspective as to the early history of St. Vincent's and providing access to documents, previously published rare accounts, out-of-print materials, and personal contacts, all of which and whom I would not otherwise have had access to (or at least not immediate accessibility). As a result, this has culminated in a most interesting and collaborative effort. One aspect that is essential to mention is that Rodger brought his concern for providing some new and appropriate perspective on the importance and treatment of the Carib Indians in relation to all these events. That was certainly a major personal desire of his, as much as it was mine to review Etherington's case in hope of supporting and revealing why he was appropriately acquitted, in addition to challenging previous conclusions about the trial which, as we have noted, were not entirely correct. (Obviously, had the evidence shown otherwise, I would have presented it and supported that conclusion as well, as hard as that might be for any author who is looking to prove or refute a point).

Neither Rodger nor I are professional historians. While that essentially makes us amateur historians, I have always been somewhat hesitant to utilize that term, since, unfortunately, some people erroneously and disrespectfully use that term and associate it in a negative connotation. In the purest sense, the term "amateur historian" means that we do not make our economic living, i.e. subsistence, as historians. Nonetheless, having been involved in such endeavors for an extended time, I have always considered myself a serious historical researcher/historian and author as a result of my nearly lifelong interest in the 18th-century British military history of Michigan, the Great Lakes area of the United States and Canada, and the American Revolution, which again obviously involved Etherington and led me on the path of research that has been previously outlined. Moreover, as several of my longtime professional historian friends and colleagues, in offering encouragement, have stated to me in the past, it is irrelevant as to whether or not a person is a *professional* historian, as anyone can make a significant and important contribution to discovering some previously unknown or unpublished aspect regarding our history and heritage that is buried somewhere in the multitude of library archives, museums and/or private collections around the world, in the effort to help preserve and share this heritage for the benefit and enjoyment of not only ourselves, but the general public as well. As such, I have always attempted to conduct and present my research within the realm of acceptable standards of the professional historian's academic circles, while bringing it to the interest of general readers of the era.

Some additional brief comments are appropriate. The resources that document the history of the British West Indies during the time of the American Revolution and before are of significant quantity and variety, ranging from in-depth studies to a more general nature concerning numerous and related topics. We have in no way attempted to present an in-depth, or for that matter, a definitive history of the British Caribbean islands and the nationalities involved, (whether military, socioeconomic aspects, or otherwise), as this has been extensively done by other historians and authors. The brief general history of St. Vincent's that we present before the trial transcripts and analysis was adapted from several of the general sources which were more inclusive of the entire Caribbean. From these, we chose to focus on and utilize those aspects pertaining specifically to St. Vincent's during this time as they related to the topic in question, for the sole purpose of placing in perspective the people, times, and events with which Etherington and Morris found themselves involved. As any author should acknowledge, we assume any and all responsibilities for factual errors contained within this publication, including those of omission. While every precaution has been taken in compiling this information, no doubt there may be some errors including those of omission. We offer our apologies for those, although we stand firm that none were intentional. We also recognize there may be differing interpretations of some or all of these events that we have presented, however, we respectively stand firm in our own interpretations and opinions on such matters. Nonetheless, the authors encourage those persons who have additional information with documentation to contact us so that changes may be considered and/or made where appropriate, if warranted, and/or debated appropriately with scholarly intent for the accepted purpose of helping to interpret and further the knowledge of the history and heritage of the era.

Finally, as is always appropriate and absolutely necessary to state, a project of this magnitude would not be possible without the assistance of many individuals and colleagues, as noted in the acknowledgments section of this book. Furthermore, it is our hope that this published history will be acceptable to interested readers and scholars, and that one can sense the true excitement and importance of these somewhat obscure events, and what it would have been like many years ago in this remote portion of the world. To that end, we hope our efforts have been successful.

Dr. Todd E. Harburn
For self and Rodger Durham
Lansing/Okemos, Michigan
June 2001

♛ ACKNOWLEDGMENTS

RECOGNITION OF CONTRIBUTIONS in the process of writing a book has been expressed in innumerable ways by countless authors before us, however, is absolutely essential and proper. As such, we would like to extend our sincere appreciation to the following individuals, institutions, and organizations for their assistance. If we have inadvertently missed anyone, it is most unintentional and greatest apologies are extended.

We are indebted in gratitude to: The Public Record Office in Kew, Richmond, Surrey, England for their gracious permission to present the previously unpublished 1781 Etherington Court Martial Trial transcripts, which provide the essence of this book, along with a photocopy of the first and last pages of these original documents. The staff at the PRO has always been most accommodating and professional in regards to this American author's (teh) inquiries and requests over the years. In particular, we would like to thank Nick Forbes, Phil Johnson, and Tim R. Padfield of the PRO Copyright Office; The Royal Green Jackets Museum (i.e. formerly the 60th or Royal American Regiment/King's Royal Rifle Corps) in Winchester, England and it's staff, Major (Retd) Ken Gray (Curator), Col. (Retd.) I.H. McCausland (former Director), and Major General Giles Mills (60th Historian) for their enthusiastic support, and moreover, their most kind permission to publish photos of the original Etherington portrait which is on permanent display at the museum; The William L. Clements Library, University of Michigan, Dr. John C. Dann, Director, and Mr. Brian L. Dunnigan, Curator of Maps, both noted historians/authors, for their kind permission to use the ca. 1831 print of Kingstown, St. Vincent's Island, the 1776 Byres map, the Lt. Charles Forrest sketches of St. Lucia, and other original documents from their famed collections as noted in the illustrations. The professionalism and courtesies extended by these gentlemen and the staff at the Clements including John Herriman, Don Wilcox and others, has always been most appreciated by this author (teh). In addition, Mr. Dunnigan's invaluable research assistance, support, encouragement, review of this manuscript, and longtime friendship over the years is greatly valued; The Richer Library, University of Miami (FL) and Ms. Ruthanne D. Vogel, Research Services and

Digital Collections Librarian, for their kind permission to use the Brunias prints from the Library's Archives and Special Collections; Mackinac State Historic Parks (MSHP), Dr. David A. Armour, Deputy Director and noted historian/author, for their kind permission to use the Gringhuis soldier print and photo of the 1770's British 60th military button, and especially for his encouragement, continued courtesies and longtime friendship (teh), special thanks also to MSHP's Mr. Steve Brisson, Curator of Collections and Mr. William Fritz, Conservator of Collections for their generosity and assistance in those endeavors in addition to MSHP Director Carl Nold and Mr. Phil Porter, Chief Curator who have been very supportive as well; The National Archives of St. Vincent's Island, Ms. Yulu Griffith, Chief Archivist and longtime friend (to rd) for her support, encouragement, research assistance, permission for map use and to quote from their collections; Dr. I. Earl Kirby, also of St. Vincent's Island, noted archaeologist/historian/author, and veterinarian, for his support, advice, and research assistance; The Cornell University Press and Mr. David Mitchell, Permissions and Marketing Assistant, for their kind permission to use the St. Vincent's map from the Craton book; The Victoria and Albert Museum of South Kensington, England and Mr. Martin Durant of the V&A Picture Library, for their kind permission to use a photo of the original 1775-76 Hearne painting contained in the Museum's collections depicting the 60th Royal Americans and government buildings at Antigua; The University of Pennsylvania Press and Mr. Francisco Aguirre, Rights and Publicity Assistant for their kind permission to use the Eastern Caribbean map from the O'Shaughnessy book; The National Portrait Gallery and Mr. Matthew Bailey, Picture Librarian, for their kind and generous permission to use the Morris portrait, and Mr. Don Troiani of Southbury, Connecticut, noted military artist/historian/collector, for his kind permission to use a photo of the later period 60th Regiment button from his extensive personal collection.

Special thanks to: Mrs. E.F. (Betty) Thomson, Professional Historical Researcher and friend (to teh) from Kew, Richmond, Surrey, England for her invaluable research assistance concerning Etherington's later career for the preceding Etherington biographical vignette and moreover, in locating the Etherington Court Martial trial transcripts (for teh); Selwyn Eagle, Professional Researcher from London, England for research assistance regarding the Morris Narratives; Tim Dubé, Military Archivist at the National Archives of Canada for his continued generosity, and meticulous professional assistance in research inquiries; Passion Tours of Bequia/St. Vincent's and the Grenadines, West Indies for their kind assistance in providing photos of the former Etherington land on St. Vincent's; Mr. Tim J. Todish of Grand Rapids, Michigan, French and Indian War/Rogers' Rangers historian/author for his support, assistance, encouragement, manuscript review, and moreover, his longtime friendship (to teh).

Others who contributed during the research and writing process, either directly or indirectly, include: Dr. Paul Huey, Archaeologist, New York State Bureau of Historic Sites, Peebles Island, NY; and Mr. Darin Flansburg, Pillager, Minnesota, a direct Etherington descendant, for sharing genealogical information (with teh) concerning Etherington for the previously mentioned vignette.

We would also be remiss in failing to mention the help of Mr. Bob Bearor of Newcomb, New York and Mr. Brent Kemmer, of Houghton Lake, Michigan, both French and Indian War historians/Heritage Books authors, historical re-enactors, and friends (of teh) for their support, encouragement, and unselfish willingness to make a recommendation to the editorial review committee at Heritage Books to consider our manuscript for publication. Without their most generous help and references, this book would not have been possible. In that regard, we must also thank the staff at Heritage Books, in particular Mrs. Leslie Wolfinger, Editorial Director, and Mrs. Roxanne Carlson, Senior Editor, for their willingness to take a chance on accepting our book for publication, and their diligent work, courtesy in accommodating the authors' requests, and professionalism throughout the publication process. We are extremely grateful to both of them.

Last but not least, to my wife Shirley and daughters Shannon and Stacey (teh), for Shirley's willingness to listen to my verbal recitations of portions of the manuscript draft and her invaluable suggestions for improvements to the same and, more importantly, for their love, support, encouragement, and perseverance during long hours spent away from them during this endeavor.

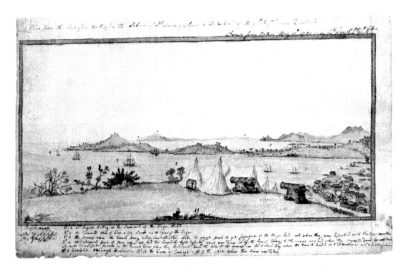

"A View from the Two Gun Battery (on the Island of St. Lucia)...May 13th 1780, Drawn from Nature by Lieutenant Charles Forrest."

This beautiful sketch with its fine detail shows the view across the bay at Carnage and the town to the right. It is unclear as to exactly where the Etherington Court Martial was held; it may have been conducted at the government buildings in the town or more likely at one of the military headquarters buildings within the huge British fort at nearby Pigeon Island. Original sketch in collections of the William L. Clements Library. Photo of same, used with permission, Courtesy: William L. Clements Library, University of Michigan.

⚜ INTRODUCTION

SITTING IN HIS QUARTERS on the Island of St. Lucia during the late hours of 4 October 1781, the evening before his court-martial trial was to begin, Lieutenant Colonel George Etherington must have wondered how he had become embodied in yet another controversy. It had been eighteen years since the loss of Fort Michilimackinac while he had been commandant there during the general Indian uprising known as Pontiac's Conspiracy that occurred in the Great Lakes region of North America in 1763, and less than half that many years since he was chastised for his manner of handling the alleged murders of Indians by a renegade fur trader during his tenure as commandant at Fort Niagara in upper New York. Yet, Etherington had since managed to rise beyond those incidents and "expunge" his record through exemplary service, enough to become appointed military commander of St. Vincent's Island in the West Indies by 1777. This trial, however, marked by bitter controversy and intended to examine his role in the loss of St. Vincent's Island to the French two years prior during the current American Revolution, was now another threat to his respected reputation. For someone who had been described as a "good and loyal officer" throughout his career in service to Great Britain, no doubt his mood was of a most melancholy nature.

The events of the American Revolution in the British Caribbean are as complex as their counterparts in the American Colonies, although they have not received as much attention by historians and the general reader until a seemingly renewed interest in recent years. They are, nonetheless, intriguing stories with each Caribbean island playing a unique role in the conflict that resulted in American Independence and the further reduction of the British Empire. The events at St. Vincent's during this time are no exception and are of particular importance as an example of the folly that occurred between military and civilian factions that ultimately contributed to the "lost" British cause.

The ignominious surrender of St. Vincent's has been the subject of several authors and historians over the years, among them Thomas Southey (1827),[1] Bryan Edwards (1794),[2] Charles Shephard (1830),[3] Dr. Thomas Edward Coke (1810),[4] Dr. Alexander

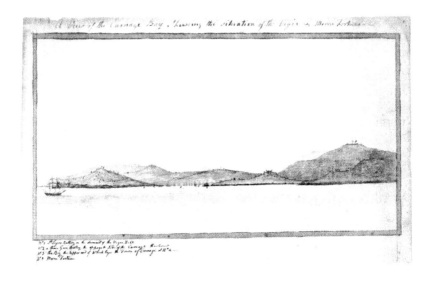

"A View of the Carnage Bay
...St. Lucia, 1780, by Lieutenant Charles Forrest."

This is a more encompassing view from a distance showing the topography of the island. Original sketch in the collections of the William L. Clements Library. Photo of same, used with permission, Courtesy of: William L. Clements Library, University of Michigan.

Anderson (1748-1812),[5] and later, Ivor Waters (1964).[6] As to the events, and the conclusions drawn from them, all are more or less in close agreement. However, the imposition of the *testimony of the witnesses* in the Etherington Court-Martial transcripts will prove, in essence, *they got it all wrong!*

The following narrative, culminating in the court-martial of Etherington, is as convoluted and complex as anyone could ever imagine, for it includes not only the American-born **Etherington**, but also the fierce **Black Caribs**, and their "War-Chief," **Chatoyer**; the governor of St. Vincent's Island, a very wealthy English aristocrat, **Valentine Morris**, Esq., born in Antigua; numerous **plantation owners** on St. Vincent's; and **The French.** As if that were not enough of a "mix," all of them were subject to the whims of the British government and the pressures brought on by the American War of Independence.

The proceedings of the trial provide many additional "behind the scenes" details about the events immediately prior to and at the surrender of St. Vincent's that were perhaps generally alluded to by the aforementioned authors, or not covered at all. In essence, it was the product of an intense personality conflict that existed between Governor Morris and Lieutenant Colonel Etherington, and both men's attempt to avoid sole blame for the surrender of the island. Moreover, a reading of the actual court-martial records will answer most of the remaining questions with respect to Etherington's actions, as will be seen. The transcript itself was previously unpublished until now and is presented here with the kind permission of the Public Record Office in Kew, England.

However, before presenting the actual account, it is not only helpful but also rather necessary to provide some background information and discussion on the principle participants in the trial and the events in the years leading up to the surrender of the island in 1779. As such, this narrative is divided into three sections; the first with respect to those just mentioned, the second containing the actual trial transcript records, and the third presenting an extensive analysis and discussion about the trial and its conclusions. The preliminary chronicle is not, however, intended as an in-depth history on the Caribbean corridor of the American Revolution (as that has already been done by other authors/historians), but rather to set the proper perspective for the fascinating St. Vincent's story.

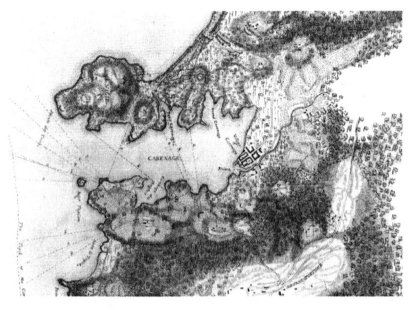

Sketch of Port of Island of St. Lucie, 1779

This map provides an overhead perspective in relation to the topographical sketches of Lt. Charles Forrest. Original map in the Lord George Germain Manuscripts, cartographic collections of the William L. Clements Library. Photo of same, used with permission, Courtesy: William L. Clements Library, University of Michigan.

⚜ PART I

THE PRINCIPLE PARTICIPANTS AND EVENTS PRIOR TO JUNE 16, 1779

(Note: Brief biographical sketches of only the three principle participants are initially presented in this section, with the epilogue of their lives contained in the final section of this book. The remaining witnesses during the trial will be mentioned and identified at the beginning of the next section, i.e. the actual trial transcript, as this provides a much easier process for the reader to follow, due to the number of participants involved.)

THE PRINCIPLE PARTICIPANTS

George Etherington (1733-after 1788?), Lieutenant Colonel, 2nd Battalion, 60th, or Royal American Regiment; British Military Commander of the Island of St. Vincent's

Born in Delaware in the American colonies, Etherington had enlisted in the British Army at a young age, first serving as a drummer and later as a sergeant major. Apparently a wealthy widow from New Castle became enamored of him and purchased him a commission as a lieutenant in the newly raised Royal American Regiment in 1756, a unit trained in "forest warfare." Thus, unlike most officers, he ascended from the ranks. He apparently had a brother, Thomas, who also later served in the 60th Regiment, although little else is known about him to date. Etherington was promoted to captain in the 1st Battalion of the regiment in 1759, apparently due to "his good reputation," an attribute which essentially summarizes his career. He distinguished himself in the French and Indian War during his various duties and assignments. He was an extremely effective recruiter for the 60th Regiment and was utilized in that capacity throughout his career, including his later tenure at St. Vincent's.

Lt. Colonel George Etherington
60th or Royal American Regiment
ca. 1773 at the Island of St. Vincent, West Indies

Portrait Attributed To: John Trotter of Dublin, Ireland, ca. 1787
Published with permission, Courtesy: The Royal Green Jackets
Museum Winchester, England

Following the conclusion of the French and Indian War, he was placed in command at Fort Michilimackinac [present Mackinaw City, Michigan, USA], one of the major British posts in the upper Great Lakes region, to maintain English fur trade interests there. In the spring of 1763, Michilimackinac was one of several forts to be captured by Indians during Pontiac's Uprising, which erupted across the wilderness frontier as relations between the British and Great Lakes Indians had deteriorated. Local Chippewa Indians attacked the post during a baggatiway contest ("Indian Lacrosse") and killed over half the garrison while taking the remaining soldiers and English traders as prisoners. Etherington and the survivors eventually made their way to safety at Montreal. Having survived this now infamous incident, Etherington went on to resume his military career.

His wife, Katy Robinson, whom he had married a year or two before the Michilimackinac mishap, apparently drowned with one of their infant daughters in a shipwreck on either Lake George or Lake Champlain in upper New York in 1763. Etherington left the other child with Colonel Philip Schuyler, a very prominent estate owner and later general in the Continental Army during the American Revolution. He continued recruiting duties for the 60th, received a promotion to major in 1770 in the 2nd Battalion, and was later appointed commandant at Fort Niagara, New York, from 1771-72. He was transferred to Antigua in 1773 with the 2nd Battalion of the 60th, which had been sent to the Caribbean to lend assistance in subduing the Carib Indians on the Island of St. Vincent's. He was instrumental in securing the peace treaty with the Caribs and as a result received a valuable land grant on the island from them, which was later to be a key factor in his dispute with Governor Morris, as will be noted. Receiving promotion to lieutenant colonel in 1775, Etherington continued in recruiting for the 60th, and presumably began plans for the eventual development of his land grant estate on the island. He was subsequently appointed military commander of St. Vincent's in October 1777 by the powerful Lord George Germain, the British Secretary of State for the American Department, due to Etherington's "considerable influence...and having gained the[ir] confidence" of the Caribs. While serving in that capacity during the next two years, the aforementioned personal feud (over the land grant as well as military policies) developed between Etherington and the governor, which led to the surrender of St. Vincent's and set the stage for the topic of the eventual General Court-Martial proceedings.

Governor Valentine Morris, Esquire

Etherington's adversary at St. Vincent Island, West Indies
From a miniature by John Smart, signed and dated 1765
Published with permission, Courtesy: The National Portrait Gallery,
London, England.

[Author's Note: The remainder of Etherington's career will be discussed in the final section of this book, as previously noted. This information was obtained during research on the first in-depth biographical sketch ever published on Etherington, which includes a color photograph of his recently discovered original portrait, published for the first time.][7]

Valentine Morris, Esquire (1727-1789)
Governor of the Island of St. Vincent's

Morris was to hold both the title of Lieutenant Governor of the Island of St. Vincent's, and later still, that of the first Governor of the Colony of St. Vincent's and the Grenadines. He was born 27 October 1727, in Antigua, in the Leeward Islands, where his family held several large sugar estates (Valentine was one of four children; Caroline, Sarah, and a brother John, 22 years older, who died in 1734). During his early childhood, his family moved back to Wales to their luxurious estate, Piercefield. At age 15, his father, Lieutenant Colonel Morris, a well-known British officer and Antigua absentee landowner, died 13 January 1742. After completing his formal schooling in 1748 at age 21, he married Mary Mordaunt, niece of the Earl of Peterborough. Despite a prohibition in his father's will that he not marry until age 25 with the penalty being the forfeiture of the estates, nothing came of it and he subsequently inherited vast wealth.

Unfortunately, he was irresponsible with his wealth and subsequently squandered it as a result of lavish expenditures at the estate, extravagant living, and gambling. In 1754, he departed Piercefield to inspect his estates in Antigua, however, he returned to Wales shortly thereafter. For the next several years until 1771, he was involved in various construction and beautification projects. In that year, he decided to run for a seat in Parliament, however, was unsuccessful. Moreover, his reputation was damaged as a result of personal character attacks making life somewhat unpleasant in England for both him and his wife. Thus, it is not surprising that in December 1772, when Lord William Dartmouth offered to appoint him Lieutenant Governor of the Island of St. Vincent's, he quickly accepted, *gratefully.*

As previously noted, he was later appointed as Governor of St. Vincent's and the Grenadines in 1776 by Lord George Germain (who had succeeded Lord Dartmouth as Secretary of State), when the people of those islands petitioned the British government for the

**Chatoyer, the Chief of the Black Charaibes
in St. Vincent with His Five Wives**

Engraving from a painting by Agostino Brunias, ca. 1770 as found in Bryan Edwards, *The History...of the British Colonies in the West Indies*, Vol. III (originally published1796), opp. page 179 of the John Stockdale 1801 edition. Print published with permission, Courtesy: Archives and Special Collections, Richter Library, University of Miami (FL)

Although little is known about Brunias during his West Indies years, nonetheless he was in close friendship with Sir William Young who owned several of his paintings depicting the Caribs and from which many engravings were made.

establishment of separate governments, apart from other nearby West Indies islands. While Morris did have good intentions for the development and further improvement of St. Vincent's, it was during his tenure as governor that he gradually alienated the plantation owners and other inhabitants due to his civil and military policies in overseeing the island. All this reached a crescendo over the next three years as the American Revolution began to involve the Caribbean Islands, and thus, the inevitable "final" clash with Etherington as earlier mentioned.[8]

Chatoyer (? 1735-1795), War Chief of the Black Caribs on the Island of St. Vincent's

"Ouboutou" (War-Chief) of the Black Caribs who inhabited St. Vincent's Island, Chatoyer was to play a prominent role in the events that determined the fate of his people in the last quarter of the 18th century. The fierce Black Caribs were descendants of the original Yellow Caribs who inhabited the islands, and African Negro slaves who were shipwrecked in 1674. Attempting to defend their homeland and way of life from encroaching Europeans, they initially fought the French during the first half of the 1700's, and still later fought several wars against the British at St. Vincent's in attempts to stop further taking of their lands. Ironically, although not surprisingly, the Black Caribs were easily influenced by and aligned with the French against the British during the American Revolution in the Caribbean corridor.

Not much is known about Chatoyer other than his involvement and leadership in the Carib wars at St. Vincent's (most notably his death, which will be discussed later). The date of his birth is not certain; one estimate is that it was in 1722, however, 1735 is more likely. It is known that he had two brothers named Dufont and DuValle, who were both Carib chiefs as well (or "Caciques" as they were known in peacetime), and later a son named John Dimmey who was tutored by the Methodist Missionary at St. Vincent's in the 1780's, eventually becoming a chief himself. Both Chatoyer and DuValle, (who was Chatoyer's "deputy"), apparently spoke French and English and the latter oversaw the Caribs on the Windward (eastern) side of the island while Chatoyer's jurisdiction was the Leeward (western) portion. Following the first Carib war in 1773, Chatoyer granted or sold large portions of land to the various British officials at St. Vincent's, although, in later years he is mentioned as having acquired additional large portions of land "assisted by loans from Englishmen for the cultivation of same...purchased slaves and was comparatively rich."

It can be surmised from what little has been written about him that Chatoyer was well respected by both Caribs and many of the British officials, yet was fierce and feared in times of conflict. As leader of his people, he was particularly involved in the Etherington-Morris events, as will be discussed.[9]

CHRONOLOGY OF EVENTS RELATING TO THE BRITISH CARIBBEAN AND THE ISLAND OF ST. VINCENT'S PRIOR TO JUNE 16, 1779

1763

The events that will bring these principle participants all together in 1781 begin in the year 1763, with the conclusion of the Seven Years' War and early reign of the English King, George III. As a result of England having defeated France, the Treaty of Paris stipulated that the Islands of Guadeloupe, Martinique, and St. Lucia were surrendered to France; Dominica, Grenada, Tobago and St. Vincent's and some minor islands comprising the Grenadines, (Bequia, Canouan Mustique, Mayreau, Union, Carriacou) were ceded to the British.[10]

Dominica, St. Lucia, and St. Vincent's (these being among the many islands collectively referred to as the Lesser Antilles; the Greater Antilles being comprised of Cuba, Jamaica, Hispaniola, and Puerto Rico) 7 February 1686, were set aside in an agreement between the two combatants as "neutral islands" in order to create a "refuge" for the Caribs.[11] Encroachment by the various European colonists in the Caribbean (Spanish, French, Dutch, and British) was forcing the native **Caribs** from their homelands, which had included all of the Windward Islands and some of the Leewards as well.[12] (The group of islands designated as the Leeward Islands were four in number; Antigua, Saint Kitts, Montserrat, and Nevis). When France ceded **St. Vincent's** along with the other aforementioned islands in November of 1763, the British intended "immediate colonization," with sale of lands to help in part subsidize the recent war,[13] and once again, not surprisingly, without regard to the Caribs.

Although officially "neutral" at St. Vincent's, French settlers had inhabited mainly the Leeward side of the island since the mid-1660's.[14] Despite having initially attempted to exterminate the

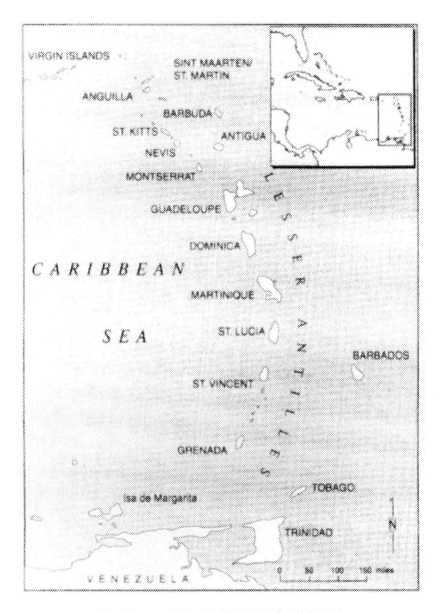

The Lesser Antilles (Eastern Caribbean)
From *An Empire Divided: The American Revolution and the British Caribbean* by Andrew J. O'Shaughnessy, Copyright ©2000 University of Pennsylvania Press. Reprinted with permission.

Caribs there, the French eventually signed a treaty and subsequently shared the island while integrating with them to some extent.[15] These original Carib Indians were known as the **Yellow Caribs**, who in turn were virtually eliminated by the **Black Caribs** during the course of the next hundred years, as will be noted. At the time of the British occupation, a survey of the inhabitants showed that there were nearly 700 French settlers, having about 3,420 slaves, and occupying nearly 7,000 acres; the total Carib population was about 3,000, and of that number, only an insignificant number, 100, were Yellow Caribs.[16]

The term **Carib** has typically been associated with the image of "cannibalistic savages," a term initiated by the Spaniards.[17] As later studies have proven, they were actually a peaceful people, yet very "fearless and hostile" when forced to defend their homeland, the latter more appropriately applied to the Black Caribs. To appreciate this perspective, it is necessary to review the difference between the indigenous Yellow Caribs and the Black Caribs with regard to their origins. The "original settlers" in the Caribbean, the "Rock People," were displaced by the "peaceful" Arawak Indians, who dominated in the region beginning about 350 A.D.[18] The latter group migrated from the northern part of South America in a series of *waves* that closely correlated with the occurrence of thermal events known as *Super Ninos* similar to the more familiar *El Ninos* of the present era. The Arawak, Lucayans in particular, were the people Columbus first encountered when he landed in the Bahamas in 1492; he discovered St. Vincent's in 1498.[19] The early Caribs (Kalinago) had also migrated to the area from South America, however, only about 100 years prior to Columbus. Both groups were similar in many of their cultural ways[20] including the color of their skin, hence the term **Yellow Caribs.** Unfortunately both native peoples would eventually be exterminated, although by somewhat different means; the Arawak quite rapidly as a result of various disease brought from Europe by the Spaniards,[21] and the Yellow Caribs much later at the hands of the Black Caribs as previously mentioned.

The **Black Caribs** are another story entirely. Their origin can be traced to the introduction of African Negro slaves by the Europeans. At St. Vincent's, this has been attributed to the wreck of a slave ship "bound for Barbados" during a hurricane in 1674 off the northeastern shore of nearby Bequia Island.[22] The survivors were rescued by the Yellow Caribs living mainly on the Leeward side of St. Vincent's, who then made them slaves of their own. Subsequently, the Africans amalgamated with the Yellow Caribs and as this "new" population increased, considerable conflict

***A Family of Charaibes, drawn from the life,
in the island of Saint Vincent***

Engraving from a painting by Agostino Brunias as found in Bryan Edwards, *History...of the British Colonies in the West Indies*, Vol. I, before page 391. Print published with permission, Courtesy: Archives and Special Collections, Richter Library, University of Miami (FL).

resulted between them and the original Yellow Caribs. These slaves, whose appearance gradually developed more to that of the black or African ethnicity, fled toward the interior mountainous parts on the Windward (Atlantic or western) side of the island. According to Sir William Young, the commissioner's son, in his book published in 1795, *An Account of the Black Charibs in the Island of St. Vincent's*, "...when the Black Caribs, (as they might properly be called at this time) fled inland &c., they were accompanied by their Yellow Carib mates and families; their numbers were quickly increased when they encountered many run-away slaves and maroons (from neighboring islands)."[23] (Maroon was the term applied to runaway slaves living in wilderness areas, particularly in Jamaica.)[24] These Black Carib communities became so numerous in the ensuing years that eventually "by 1763, the Yellow Caribs were reduced to insignificance."[25]

As a people, the Black Caribs were "educated, not simply ignorant savages" which was a combined result of their interaction with white Europeans as well as their cultural ancestry. While continuing a loose affiliation with the French and speaking that language, they also maintained their sophisticated social and tribal life.[26] Yet, they had a tendency for devastating destruction of life and property, torture/atrocities, and were well suited to guerilla warfare in the heavy terrain of St. Vincent's while defending their homeland. As such they were considered much more fierce and capable of inflicting terror upon their enemies than their predecessors. In these aspects, the British completely underestimated them and would realize they were "a force to be reckoned with" during the warfare that would erupt in later years.[27]

Socially, the Caribs lived in small communal units, each governed by a cacique, or chief.[28] In time of war, however, all the Caribs temporarily united under one "war-chief" (ouboutou). At this time, and for years to come in St. Vincent's, that chief was **Chatoyer**.

1764

In England in 1764, the Commission to Oversee Land Redistribution and Sales was established, and arrangements for a survey were made.[29] Sir William Young, Robert Stuart and Robert Wynne were designated as commissioners, and later Robert Stuart was replaced by M. Hewitt. Sir William was designated chief commissioner. In March, a proclamation was issued for the sale of all His Majesty's lands in Grenada, the Grenadines, Dominica, St. Vincent's, and Tobago. Purchasers were required to pay twenty per cent deposit and to pay off the remainder with a succession of equal payments, along with other various requirements.[30] Land purchase was limited to five hundred acres,[31] except in Dominica, where it was limited to three hundred. "Sixpence was to be paid as a *quit-rent* for cleared lands" and, in addition, stipulations were made for the establishment of towns and other land use.[32]

At this time, while still resident in England, Sir William Young published an essay entitled, *Encouraging Adventurers to Embark Their Fortunes and Industry in the New Islands*, in which he recommended the "Fertile Soil" of St. Vincent's. Young also remarked "on the intentions of the British Government with regard to the Black Caribs...that when the Black Caribs of St. Vincent's are duly apprised of the Humanity and Generosity of our Gracious Sovereign, and Assured of the Enjoyment of their lands, Freedom, Favour, and Protection, they may be gained over to our cause, and even rendered useful."[33] Unfortunately for the Black Caribs, this never came to fruition, and a continuous dispute over land ownership and distribution would develop of the next several years.

This situation was typical of the British government's arrogance and policies with respect to the acquisition of lands throughout its world empire, as evidenced by a similar parallel attitude toward the various native tribes of the Great Lakes area in North America during this same time. Despite the stated intentions, whether "co-habitation" with the Caribs at St. Vincent's was to be by the purchase and/or granting of land from them, the blatant and outright taking of the lands by the British was essentially the end result. Moreover, this disingenuous handling of such transactions tangentially occurred toward its own arriving colonists, as the British government even disregarded the aforementioned limitations on the amount of land allowed to be acquired by immediately granting 4000 acres to General Robert Monckton, (British commander of the recent victory at Havana, Cuba in 1762), and another 20,000 acres to a Mr. Swineburne.[34]

The underlying incentive to all this was, of course, (aside from the government's desire to help recover costs for the recent Seven Years' War) the driving prospect of making enormous wealth via sugar plantations, particularly since the Caribs held the prime land portions for this specific crop (which would become one of the main exports in the West Indies, as is well known in history). This was most evident by the tremendous influx of British colonists from other British islands and North America, as well as the government's

A View of Kingstown, St. Vincent, ca. 1831.

The town is similar to its appearance in 1779. Photo reprinted with permission, Courtesy: William L. Clements Library, University of Michigan.

immediate auction in 1764 of the remaining lands to these incoming people. The population of St. Vincent's more than doubled in less than one year; in 1763 it was listed as having "695 white men, 1138 free Negroes, and 3430 slaves" and "2104 Whites, and 7414 Slaves" the following year.[35]

Late in the year, following Young's recommendations regarding "Treatment to be Accorded to the Charaibs," the British government issued a statement in temporarily restraining any "Survey...of Lands Occupied or Claimed by the Charaibs until further Instructions."[36]

1765

St. Vincent's, as it was then known—St. Vincent, today—is a small to medium size island, being only about 133 square miles in area, 18 1/2 miles long, running generally north and south, and 11 1/4 miles wide.[37] The principle town, now, as then, is Kingstown, which is situated on the southwestern coast overlooking a large bay that "affords good protection and most excellent anchorage." Only about one-third of the island is suitable for agriculture due to the ruggedness of the terrain and the semi-active volcano called Soufriere, which is located in the northern portion. In 1765, Kingstown consisted only of three main streets which ran parallel to the water, and six cross streets. At the time, there were very few houses, but what there were, were all gaily painted in yellows, blues and pinks, most having red roofs.[38] Soon, upon the arrival of the British, an Anglican church and fortifications were constructed for defense of the town. The latter included a small fort (barracks) on Berkshire Hill (later expanded as Fort Charlotte in 1806) to the west of town, a battery opposing it on the east side of the bay on what was to become known as Mr. Hartley's Hill (Sion Hill) and another more substantive battery above the town, on Dorchester Hill.[39] Visitors to the island proclaimed it as "being the most beautiful and healthful Island in the Caribbean," as many still do today.

It soon became obvious to the aforementioned land commissioners that the Carib situation would be a more difficult "problem" to resolve than at first envisioned, in part, due to the continued influence and association of the French government with the natives. As such, a "Publick Agent" named Abbe' Valladares, was employed to negotiate and possibly arrive at some type of "arrangement" with them.[40] This failed, in part, because the commissioners disregarded the individual Carib factions with respect to their political and cultural organization by attempting to deal with only one tribal leader, and moreover, because the Caribs simply refused to acknowledge allegiance to the British Crown. In response to this, the commissioners made recommendations in August of 1765 to the Treasury authorities in England for a proposal to offer the Caribs "resettlement on the nearby Island of Bequia," although this was later withdrawn.[41]

Thereafter, the arrival of plantation owners and colonists was not slowing and despite the political dispute that was occurring, the Caribs were pressured to continue to allow "grants" and the appropriation of their "unoccupied" lands on the island, the latter of which the French inhabitants were also subjected.

Also in the same year, General Robert Melville took his place as Governor of the Lesser Antilles. The title of **Governor** in the islands then was quite different from what it would connote today, both with respect to *responsibility and power*. Because one of the principle characters in the narrative, **Valentine Morris**, was to accede to this office, it is well to learn more about it. Brian Edwards, an Antiguan planter and historian writing in 1794, offers the following:

Governor

Every Chief Governor in the British West Indies is appointed by Letters of Patent under the Great Seal of Great Britain. He receives, through courtesy, the Title of Excellency, and is vested with the following powers:

First, as Captain-General and Commander in Chief, he has the actual command of all the Land Forces within his Government (the exception being when a general Officer is employed on the staff) and he commissions all Officers of the Militia. He appoints the Judges of all the different Courts of Common Law, and even these Gentlemen, in all the islands (with the exception of Jamaica) hold their seats during the Governor's good pleasure. He nominates and supersedes, at will, the custodies of the several Parishes, Justices of the Peace, and other subordinate Civil Officers; and although, in respect to some of the above appointments and demissions, he is directed to ask the advice of his Council. This "direction" is of little avail, inasmuch as the members of this body are themselves liable to be suspended by the Governor, on the most frivolous pretenses, or even without any cause assigned; a circumstance, by the way, which not infrequently happens; and having thus reduced the Board under a number limited by his instructions, he can fill up the vacancies *instanter*, with such persons as will be "proper obedient."

He has the authority, with the advice of his Council, to summon General Assemblies; He appoints the place of their meeting, and when met, he possesses a negative voice in the Legislature, for without his consent, no Bill passes into a Law; and he may, from time to time, as he along shall judge needful, adjourn, prorogue, and dissolve all such General Assemblies. He has the authority to depose of all such Civil Employments as the Crown does not dispose of; and with respect to such Offices as are usually filled up by the British Government, if vacancies happen, the Governor appoints "pro tempore," and the persons so appointed are entitled to all the emoluments, until they are superseded at home, and until the persons nominated to supersede them, arrive in the Colony. The Governor claims the privilege also, in extraordinary cases, and has been known frequently to exercise it, of suspending such Civil Officers even as act immediately under the King's Authority, or by Commission from Boards of Treasury and Admiralty, in high and lucrative employments, as the Attorney and Advocate-General, the Collectors of the Customs, &c., and nominating other persons to act in their room, until the King's pleasure shall be known therein. To all which is added Authority, when he shall judge any offender in criminal matters a fit object of mercy, to extend the King's Gracious Pardon towards him, except only in cases of murder and high treason; and even in these cases, the Governor is permitted to reprieve until the signification of the Royal Pleasure.

Secondly, the Governor has the custody of the Great Seal, and, in most of the Colonies, presides solely in the High Court of Chancery. Indeed, in some of the Windward Islands, as we have seen, the Council sit as Judges in the Court of Chancery with the Governor: Process, however, is issued by the Governor alone, and tested in his name; and in general, the Governor exercises with his jurisdiction, the same extensive powers as are possessed by the Lord High Chancellor of Great Britain.

Thirdly, the Governor is Ordinary, and collates to all vacant Church benefices. He hath also the power of granting Probate of Wills, and Administration of the effects of persons dying in testate. He grants licenses for marriages, and licenses for schools, &c. and is sole Judge in all matters relating to Consistorial or Ecclesiastical Law.

Fourthly, the Governor presides in the Court of Error, of which he and the Council are Judges, to hear and determine all appeals, in the nature of Writs of Error, from the Superior Courts of Common Law.

Fifthly, the Governor was also the Vice-Admiral within the extent of his Government. As such, he was entitled to the rights of "Jetsan" and "Flotsam," &c. and in time of War, he is entitled to issue his Warrant to the Judge of the Court of Vice-Admiralty, to grant Commissions to Privateers.

Lastly, A Colony-Governor, besides various emoluments arising from fees, fines, forfeitures, and escheats, has an Honourable Annual Provision settled upon him, By Act of Assembly, for the whole term of his Administration in the Colony. For, in order that he may not be tempted to prostitute the dignity of his station by improper Condescension's to leading men in the Assembly, he is restrained by his instructions from accepting any salary, unless the same be settled upon him by law.[42]

Lieutenant General, Lieutenant Governor, and President

In a Government comprehending several Islands, as that of the Leeward Caribbean Islands, there is commonly appointed, together with the Captain-General or Chief-Governor, a Lieutenant-Governor likewise of one of the Islands included within the General Government, each of which, in the absence of the Captain-General from that particular Island, has its affairs administered by a Lieutenant-Governor, or the President of the Council, most commonly the latter, as it is not often that the Lieutenant-Governor is on the spot; this appointment, in fact, being nothing more that the Grant of a Pension of £200 a year, which is paid by the Crown. On the resignation, or absence on leave, of the Captain-General, a Lieutenant-Governor, if not present, is frequently sent over, who then succeeds to the Supreme Command, and receives the full emoluments of the Government. A President of the Council, taking upon him the

Government on the demise or absence of a Governor or Lieutenant-Governor, cannot legally dissolve the House of Assembly, nor issue Writs for calling a new one; because he has no express commission from the Sovereign under the Great Seal of Great Britain, giving authority for that purpose.[43]

Valentine Morris, Esq., as previously mentioned, was later to hold both the title of Lieutenant Governor of the Island of St. Vincent's, and later still, that of the first Governor of the Colony of St. Vincent's and the Grenadines.

1765 was also the year that the infamous Stamp Act was passed by the British government on all its colonies; yet another means in which to help raise revenue to pay for debt remaining from the Seven Years' War. This act, which taxed all sorts of public documents, land conveyances, commissions and licenses, newspapers, etc., was annoying, but not critical. It is not intended to relate the consequences in detail concerning the history of this enactment, as that has been well documented and discussed by many other historians.[44] However, for purposes of this discussion, suffice to say that the Caribbean colonies felt the effects of this act harder than their North American counterparts for a variety of reasons, which included a different rate of taxation on promissory notes and bonds, particularly of concern at St. Vincent's (as well as Tobago, Dominica, and Grenada) in view of the land dealings, and a shortage of coin currency in the Caribbean, as cash payment was required on these duties.[45] Although the Stamp Act was repealed the following year, tensions eventually escalated into the American Revolution in the North American colonies. In the Caribbean, though, more concern was directed to the fact that "evasions" of the edict were under the auspices of the Vice-Admiralty Courts, thus "denying the right to trial by jury."

1766-1767

The land commissioners and the Caribs remained at a stalemate with the former group in a dilemma as to "what manner to proceed" in order to find a solution that would be acceptable to all the parties involved (the Caribs, French inhabitants, British colonists, and Negro slaves) yet maintain the "Rights of the Crown." In the meantime, a steady inflow of colonists, plantation owners, and absentee landowners continued to "use every ruse imaginable to obtain lands" at St. Vincent's which further inflamed the entire situation. By the end of 1766, this consolidated effort further sustained the commissioners' intent to "make St. Vincent's second only to Jamaica among British sugar colonies" with St. Vincent's having surpassed Dominica by threefold in total export of produce.[46] Three years prior in 1764, this was recorded for St. Vincent's to be "12,000 andoulles of tobacco, 7,900 cwts. of cocoa, and 14,700 cwts. of coffee."[47]

Of additional concern in St. Vincent's at this time was political policy and management of the slave population. Throughout the West Indies, irrespective of nationality (i.e., French, British, Dutch or Spanish), the colonial governments saw a continuing increase in the number of slaves owing to the need for sustaining the export of agricultural commodities from the plantations. As in the American colonies, slaves were considered inferior in status and the difference between the "European sector and the Negroe sector" was extreme.[48] At St. Vincent's, this was most evident by passage of the Act of 1767 which set a multitude of stipulations for civil law concerning slaves, among these, "declaring slaves to be real estate."[49] Some progress was made, albeit minimal, in regards to free Negroes and Mulattoes who were allowed to own no more that eight acres although as "non-freeholders" (i.e. lack of political rights).[50] Similar to the Caribs, although obviously involving a slightly different etiology, a means of resistance for the slaves was a revolt. As such, major slave revolts were not uncommon in the West Indies, yet none occurred at St. Vincent's. While no less important to Caribbean history, analysis of the various maroon and slave revolts against "white colonialism" is beyond the focus of this present discussion and has been covered much more extensively by numerous authors and historians.[51]

Also worthy of mention in 1767 is that at the Island of St. Vincent's, an historic event took place—the inauguration of the Botanic Gardens. "The Gardens," modeled after the famed one at Kew in England, was the *first* in the Western Hemisphere and came, over time, to be regarded as among the best in the world. General Melville, still Governor of the Lesser Antilles, prevailed upon St. Vincent's Hospital surgeon **Doctor George Young** to take up the task of its development and act as curator.[52] Dr. Young will later reappear as the defense's only witness.

1768-1769

Since the Carib land dispute still remained, at the request of the authorities in England, Chief Commissioner Sir William Young made recommendations, which were accepted for the long awaited "Instructions" promised four years prior. These were distributed throughout St. Vincent's in May and were as follows:

I. That the Commissioners shall survey and dispose of all the cultivated lands from Ribichi (Rabacca) to Grand Sable, and round to Chatteau-Bellair (Chateaubellair).

II. That no step shall be taken towards the removal of any Charaib, 'till the whole arrangement and design shall have been notified, and explained, to the satisfaction of the Chiefs; and they be made to comprehend the conditions on which the Settlement was proposed, and that the plan be carried into effect with the gentlest hand, and in the mildest manner.

III. That in fixing the Quarter of the Island destined for the New Settlement, every proper indulgence be shown them, and that the lands allotted for them, in exchange, be convenient for their habitation, sufficient for their support, and, in point of situation, adapted to their manner of living.

IV. Certificates shall be given to their principle persons of the situation and quantity of land allotted to them.

V. The absolute property of the lands so allotted, shall be assured to them and their children, and in such a manner as shall be found most to their satisfaction, and agreeable to their customs.

VI. They shall have gathered in their provisions from their former lands, and built houses on their lands newly allotted, they shall be permitted to remain in their former situation, and five years shall be allowed them for these purposes.

VII. Under the terms, the spots of cleared land they now occupy shall be sold, and made part of Plantation Allotments, with the woodlands, which surround them; and on the final removal of the Charaibs shall make part of such property.

VIII. Such spots of cleared land shall be sold at not less than £10, the acre; to be paid in two payments, one half down, the other at the expiration of five years.

IX.X. Of the purchase money for such cleared land, 4 Joannes, or £8 Sterling per acre, shall be paid to the Charaibs who claim the lands, and be paid to the Charaibs in two equal payments, one half at time of sale, and the other moiety in five years; or sooner, on certificate of his removal to lands allotted for him in exchange.

XI. If at the end of five years, the Charaib shall not have prepared for removal, or built him a hut on the new lands allotted him, the Governor, &c. may and shall direct the Planter, succeeding to the land, to build a hut for the said Charaib, accounting for the residue of the Purchase Money due to him.

XII. No *quit-rent* shall be reserved for lands allotted to the Charaibs, but they shall be the absolute property of them and their descendents, or assigns, provided always that they may not alienate to any White Person.

XIII. If in the course of the arrangement, the remains of the Native, or Red Charaibs, desire for their security, to be separated and settled apart from the free Negroes, it shall be done. (The term *Red Charaib* came into use at this time to differentiate the Charibs from the East Indians)

XIV. Returns to be made of the Charaibs, who receive allotments and take the Oath of Fidelity to the King.

XV. No fee whatever to be taken for Charaib allotments.[53]

The previously mentioned public agent, Abbe' Valladares, was sent out by the commissioners to make a tour of the Carib country and explain the instructions in hopes that they would be accepted. The Caribs, not surprisingly, declined. (Valladares was later threatened, his nephew and black servant both killed and his housed burned).[54]
Despite this, early in 1769, the British were able to complete construction of a road through the Carib lands during the survey. Following this, they sent forty troops under the command of Captain **Wilkie** (a name later to appear in the court-martial), to take possession of the post where the surveyors had sheltered, the latter

having left the area being "terrified at the Caribs." Three hundred armed Caribs then surrounded the post, although through the efforts of Captain Wilkie no hostilities erupted and his detachment returned safely along with a contingent of armed settlers who had joined them to help if necessary. The Caribs destroyed the roads and temporary huts at the post.[55]

The commissioners were now receiving repeated accounts of predatory attacks on different plantation settlements in the outlying country, that slaves were being carried off and sold to the French, and that the Caribs had been in contact with the French governor of Martinique.[56]

By 17 July 1769, both the commissioners and plantation owners were petitioning the British government with letters to Secretary of State, the Earl of Hillsborough, for the use of "force...to reduce the Charaibs."[57] However, this was not to be undertaken for another three years.

1770-1771

Nothing of consequence occurred during 1770 aside from the fact that the "pleadings" for removal of the Caribs from the island became increasingly more frequent and stern to the authorities in England. As no action was taken, an "innovative scheme was... concocted by...certain Adventurers" whereby British government officials would be offered "silent partnerships" in land companies as a means to entice their support for acquiring the lands.[58] This failed to materialize, however.

On 2 March 1771, General William Leyborne Leyborne, Esq. was appointed Captain-General and Governor-in-Chief of the Southern Caribbee Islands replacing Brigadier-General Robert Melville.[59] Dominica was set aside as a separate colony and Sir William Young was appointed its governor, leaving his position as chief commissioner at St. Vincent's.

In an attempt to placate the situation, the British government announced previously on 2 January 1771 that all "Fraudulent-Purchases were annulled."[60] However, the Caribs absolutely rejected this and reiterated that "they were *Independent* of the Kings, of either France or England," although observing that they would continue to favor and align themselves with the French, who continued to encourage the natives to resist. The land commissioners, by July, had totally lost patience with the Caribs and

**The 60th or Royal American Regiment
shown mounting an honor guard for Governor Sir Ralph Payne
of Antigua 1775 at St John's, Antigua.**

The 60th had been sent to the West Indies in late 1772 to assist in the Carib War at St. Vincent Island. They were initially stationed at Antigua and later St. Vincent Island during the American Revolution from 1776-79. Original painting entitled *Court House and Guard House in the Town of St. John's, Antigua*, by Thomas Hearne, 1775-76. Published with permission, Courtesy: Victoria and Albert Museum, South Kensington, England.

finally agreed with the plantation owners and other colonists that military action was necessary.

1772

Since the Caribs remained obstinate in refusing allegiance to His Sovereign Majesty King George III, the British government on 18 April 1772 passed motions approving an expedition against the Caribs.[61] It was decided to send two regiments of troops from North America to join those already in garrison at St. Vincent's to deal with them. The troops initially involved in the campaign included the 14th, 31st, 32nd, 60th, and 70th Regiments totaling some 1596 men,[62] with the 32nd Regiment having been stationed on St. Vincent's since 1765.[63] They were, however, eventually joined by the 6th, 50th, and 68th Regiments, and an additional 165 men of the 60th Regiment, to which **Etherington** was attached, having arrived in Antigua from North America by January 1773 late in the war. These units, along with contingents of the Marines and Royal Artillery thus increased the total troops to 2,273.[64] The objective of the campaign was to "reduce the Caribbs to a due submission ...or...that they might be removed from the island..." yet "...treated with all imaginable humanity in their passage."[65] The commanding officer, Major General William Dalrymple, and a portion of the new troops were not able to arrive until the 30th of August, and it was another month before the remaining regiments were assembled and the expedition ready to begin.[66]

The British were quite mistaken in hoping for a quick end to the war and reluctant in eventually acknowledging that the Caribs were a *very tough opponent*. Not only had the campaign begun at the "unhealthy season of the year" —the rainy season—but the British also underestimated the Caribs' proficiency in "guerilla warfare" within thick mountainous terrain; both factors contributing heavily to casualties. Despite General Dalrymple's optimism that these aspects would "be overcome by our utmost diligence & perseverance,"[67] the troops encountered much difficulty and had advanced only four miles into Carib lands by mid November.[68]

In England at this time, Lord Dartmouth, recently appointed Minister of Trade and Plantations, appointed **Valentine Morris, Esq.** to be Lieutenant-Governor of the Island of St. Vincent's, under the command of Governor Leyborne Leyborne.

1773

It was not until 25 January 1773 that the Caribs finally sought a "parley" with the British. This was in part due to the failure of assistance from the French although the Caribs were still opposed to overt submission. The British, on the other hand, were most anxious to end the war as well due to the casualties and the stalemate that had ensued. General Dalrymple's official return of casualties for the entire campaign reported, "72 killed, 83 wounded, 110 deceased (due to the climate), 4 desertions, and 428 sick (in the hospital).[69] Moreover, public sentiment back in England eventually had become favorable to the Caribs for a variety of reasons including human rights issues, "national character," and the aforementioned problems of fighting a war in a difficult terrain and climate (heavy forested mountains, extreme temperatures, and torrential rains).

When the negotiations were entered into, it immediately came to light that none of the English officers spoke French, with the exception of **Major George Etherington.** He was ordered to take charge of the negotiations and he set about the task with several of the Carib chiefs, among them, the "war-chief," **Chatoyer.** Most likely, *during the lengthy discussions*, Etherington was able to enter into an agreement with the Caribs for his personal purchase of lands within the Carib boundary, as to have done so after the Treaty was concluded would have required, by the Articles of the Peace, for him to have obtained permission from the government. Some officers did petition the British House of Commons after the war for consideration of granting and/or sale of lands; however, no evidence to date has been found to indicate Etherington was among this group.[70] He eventually did seek approval from the British Treasury Board in 1776 (only after being declined by Morris), and the fact that he was never challenged by the Caribs regarding it, suggests this is the case (although some questions remain with regards to this, as will be later discussed). The treaty was finally completed and signed on 27 February 1773 and published in the *St. Vincent's Gazette.* It was signed by twenty-eight Carib chiefs, including **Chatoyer.**[71]

Inasmuch as Etherington's estate becomes a factor in the court-martial, it is worthwhile learning more about it. The estate was "enormous," being about 1,000 acres, about 1/32 of the entire available agricultural land on the island. It was located on the Wallibou River, some eighteen to twenty-three miles from Kingstown, on the Leeward (northwest) side of the island. Quite suited for sugar cane production, this later to be borne out when the estate was divided into halves and sold, subsequently being put to that purpose; however, Etherington was never to produce any. According to Brian Edwards' *History, Civil and Commercial in the British Colonies in the West Indies*, [Vol. II] one would have to be "very, very wealthy" to afford the investment required to establish a sugar plantation and put it into production, Edwards estimating the investment, given a *moderate* estate size, at £30,000.

That Etherington's legal right to the estate was widely recognized is borne out by the fact that it is noted on the Crown Surveyor's map of St. Vincent's, dated 1776. The Crown Surveyor, **John Byres,** will also be mentioned in the course of the court-martial proceedings. In addition, a most likely assumption is that he was a close friend of Etherington, as Byres' map of Bequia is dedicated to him. By this time Etherington had received a promotion to the rank of lieutenant colonel in the 2nd Battalion of the 60th at Antigua. In 1779, Etherington's ownership was confirmed, when the Lords of the Treasury affixed the Great Seal to his deed.

Sir William Young (son) wrote, "The Treaty was essentially those propositions originally suggested by the Commissioners...and defined...in respect to the Crown...their relative Duties and Rights, Allegiance and Protection."[72] However, another observer wrote that "it was a *Charade"* since the Caribs neither fully understood English law nor spoke the language well. Obviously, as was the usual practice, the treaty was skewered to favor the British interests, and although the Caribs were now "officially" subjects of the Crown, they in essence still considered themselves independent, and rightly so.

However, it should also be noted that in this same year, Sir William himself, had acquired a very large tract of good land on the southern Leeward Side of the St. Vincent's from Chatoyer. The story related as to how this came to be was that "having met Chatoyer on the road one day and giving him two magnificent white horses..." the Carib chief "in turn...told him to take it, if you so desire" pointing to the area in question.[73] This estate totaled about 1000 acres (Pembroke and Villa Estates] and included present day Young's Island, a small island just a short distance off the southern beaches of St. Vincent's. This is somewhat ironic, as Young had been involved in the selling off of properties while serving as the first commissioner, as previously noted.

Valentine Morris, on his way to take up his post as lieutenant governor in St. Vincent's, stopped at Antigua to do business in his estates. While there, he learned that the governor, Leyborne Leyborne, had died, and immediately expressed a letter to Lord

Engraving depicting the **Signing of the February 1773 Treaty Between the British and the Black Caribs at St. Vincent Island**; later printings of this engraving were erroneously entitled *An Historical Survey of the Island of Saint Domingo, together with an Account of the Maroon Negroes in the Island of Jamaica.*

In reality the illustration at left depicts the treaty negotiations and signing between Chatoyer and his fellow chiefs of the Black Caribs and General William Dalrymple. Chatoyer is shown in the center with General Dalrymple seated. Also, while not proven, it is nonetheless highly possible that Lt. Col. Etherington is depicted next to the officer holding the formal documents of the treaty since he was highly involved in the negotiation of the treaty terms and as suggested by the dark facings of his regimental coat (the 60th had dark blue facings) and a potential (albeit slight) resemblance to his later painted original portrait. Engraving from an original painting by Agostino Brunias ca. 1775 as found in Bryan Edwards, *History...of the British Colonies in the West Indies*, Vol. III, between pages 310 and 311. Print published with permission, Courtesy: Archives and Special Collections, Richter Library, University of Miami (FL).

Lt. Col. Etherington's Land Grant as it appeared in 1999 on St. Vincent Island, West Indies.

Photo, Co-author's collections, taken for the authors by and Courtesy of: Passion Tours, Inc., Bequia Island, St. Vincent and the Grenadines.

Dartmouth to be named the governor's replacement. In this request, he was supported in a letter sent by Sir William Young to Lord Dartmouth, who noted that Morris's father "served the Crown for nearly forty years in the Army, with singular honour and reputation," and it was only fitting that his son's request be granted. However, due to both his wife's and his own illnesses, Morris was unable to proceed to St. Vincent's until early the next year. Additionally, while recuperating in Antigua, he made the suggestion to Lord Dartmouth that St. Vincent's, and the more northerly of the Grenadines, should be made a separate government from Grenada, as they were too far distant from there to be properly attended to.

·1774

During this time in North America, the situation regarding the disagreements over Great Britain's governmental policies affecting the colonies there had become more intense. Substantial trade had developed between the British West Indies and the American colonies for amenities that both saw as necessary for their economies. The West Indies were able to obtain food "especially salt fish and corn" to feed the slave populations, whereas their North American counterparts received desirable items such as "rum and molasses" and, of course, sugar.[74] While this benefited both groups, nonetheless, in reality it was more advantageous to Great Britain since it received the "tax and duty" revenue from all these transactions.

Despite disagreements with the American colonies in earlier years as to some of the Crown policies by the British Caribbean islands, whose tendency had been more favorable toward Great Britain, there was great concern among the latter about the probable cessation of trade that might occur in the event of an American rebellion. This became a reality when the Continental Congress disallowed such activity in 1774.[75]

At St. Vincent's, newly appointed Governor Morris had arrived in late 1774, and it was obvious from the onset that his tenure as governor would be a tenuous one. He immediately alienated the Assembly there by inflammatory and arrogant statements directed toward them, which he described as "a turbulent Colony, little disposed to conduct itself with Order and Regularity, or to pay due respect to Proper Authority,"[76] and that there were "three or four inconsiderate Members who…promoted Opposition" to all policies recommended by the governor. These sorts of statements obviously made him most unpopular among his constituents and the Assembly. This was further agitated when he publicly supported the French inhabitants because of their work ethic and appreciation of land (as opposed to the plantation owners) and proposed their "unrestricted access to settle in the Island." A subsequent bill by the Assembly to classify the majority of French inhabitants as "vagrants" was defeated in a vote, and many of the French families moved to the nearby islands of St. Lucia and Martinique which were more receptive to their presence in contrast to the British plantation owners and colonists of St. Vincent's.[77]

In addition to the antagonistic relationship with the Assembly, the other equally serious problem that would plague Governor Morris for the remainder of his term was the Carib situation. As a result of the 1773 treaty, they had been granted the northern half of the island, which contained the best lands for plantations, particularly the growing of sugar as well as coffee, the latter crop being what most of the French inhabitants had developed over the years. Again, as in the years preceding the 1773 insurrection, the local British officials (which would include the Governor himself) saw this as a prime opportunity to make their fortunes and further develop the island in the process, despite their disagreements with their new governor. Almost immediately at the onset of his taking office, the Caribs were pressured into parting with additional lands. Although some of these transactions were by their choice, others were not and the Caribs also complained about lands being acquired beyond the agreed boundaries in violation of the treaty agreement by greedy opportunists among the colonists.

Morris was faced with trying to appease both sides while implementing his plan for the island's development and military defense as well. Such projects included the building of roads further into the island and the establishment of military posts for peacekeeping purposes. Both of these were to prove most difficult as the Caribs continued to engage in occasional violent activity such as raiding plantations, harassing settlers, and harboring runaway slaves, all of which eventually raised fears of a potential Carib-slave uprising against the colonists.[78] In reality, however, these aspects are understandable and not unexpected since the Caribs were merely defending their homelands and their way of life, and never relinquished their autonomy.

1775-1776

Little of consequence happened throughout 1775 at St. Vincent's. The Carib situation remained somewhat docile for the most part while the Assembly and inhabitants continued their "bantering" over the island's politics. Of interesting note, however, is that Sir William Young resigned as Governor of Dominica,[79] and returned to St. Vincent's where he would reside in future years.

In March of 1776, the new Secretary of State for the American Department in Colonial Affairs, Lord George Germain, appointed Valentine Morris as the first Governor of St. Vincent's and its Dependent Islands, with the additional titles of Captain-General, Commander-in-Chief and Vice-Admiral, after the islands had been granted separate jurisdiction from Grenada because of the "Charaib troubles," which Morris had requested four years earlier of Lord Dartmouth.[80] Not surprisingly, the inhabitants and the Assembly were less than enthusiastic with this new development. Their opposition to a plethora of issues and events that surrounded governor Morris's administration further increased and would develop into a struggle of epic proportions between both sides.

The American colonies' declaring their Independence in July of 1776 and the beginning of hostilities there, indeed posed new problems for St. Vincent's and its fellow British West Indies colonies. Aside from the disruption in trade, which had ceased two years earlier as noted, there was also intense concern regarding possible French involvement in the war and actual invasion of the islands. While the French did not immediately "officially" join the American cause, they were involved in assisting with military supplies (particularly gunpowder) from their Caribbean islands.[81] American privateers and merchant ships began infiltrating the West Indies, the most notable being William Bingham in Martinique, who established a trade network throughout the French islands which caused further difficulties among the various plantation owners and colonists in obtaining their necessities from England, since their own North American sources had been disrupted.[82] Moreover, the French and Caribs assisted privateers, and the result of all these activities was to further many of the Caribbean inhabitants to be sympathetic to the Americans. In particular at St. Vincent's, Governor Morris had suspicions that some plantation owners and commissioners had sympathies toward the American cause and might start a civil insurrection of their own, which added to the already present tension over a possible French invasion. He specifically singled out former Lieutenant Governor and present Speaker of the Assembly,

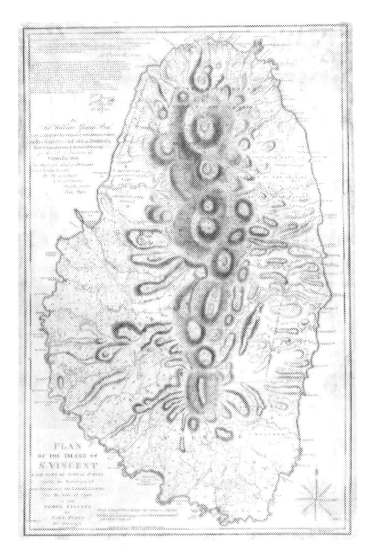

Plan of the Island of St. Vincent laid down by Actual Survey under the Direction of Honorable Commissioners for the Sale of Lands in the Ceded Islands, by John Byres, Chief Surveyor, 1776.

Map, one of several originals in collections of the William L. Clements Library. Photo of same, used with permission, Courtesy: William L. Clements Library, University of Michigan.

Henry Sharpe, and his brother, Charles Payne Sharpe, who was married to Morris's niece.[83]

Underlying these other diversions, however, was the Carib problem, which had never been resolved. It was also during 1776 that the commissioners and Assembly had proceeded with the aforementioned Byres' survey of the island for the purposes of recognizing various land claims and plantations as well as for the sales of new Carib lands. The Caribs were complaining of land acquisitions beyond the 1773 treaty boundaries, although there is some question that they had, at times, been involved in authorizing and/or making such transactions. Moreover, they continued to harass inhabitants and plantation owners near the border boundaries with their lands. From the beginning of his term, Governor Morris had attempted to deal with this problem. While in reality he was not entirely supportive of the Carib cause or their right to retain their land at St. Vincent's, he, on the other hand, intended for further island development and did not want this to occur in such a blatant and outright visible manner. He initially encouraged the purchase of small tracts of less than fifty acres by families near the Carib boundary with the ulterior motive being that by having these estates near the island's small fortified posts in the outlying country, it would assist in both supplying the posts as well as (hopefully) improving relations with the more friendly factions of the Caribs.[84]

He, however, opposed the sale of lands to individuals, although he had actually subversively made arrangements for members of his own family to purchase land "grants," which was later addressed by Lord Germain, as will be discussed. In fact, he had even accused "Major Etherington, Commissary Walker, and Charles Sharpe (his nephew-in-law)" of illegally buying land from the Caribs after persuading them to sell and having this approved by the Assembly during one of the Governor's absences from St. Vincent's, visiting a nearby island[85] about the time of the aforementioned Byres' survey.

1777

The continuous tangential issue overlying the politics at St. Vincent's was the defense of the island against a French invasion. Early in this year, Great Britain was in the extreme predicament in that it lacked the resources to not only fight the Revolution in North America, but also, properly defend its Caribbean islands as well. What few troops there were in St. Vincent's were ordered to North America; they numbered four companies of the 32nd Regiment,

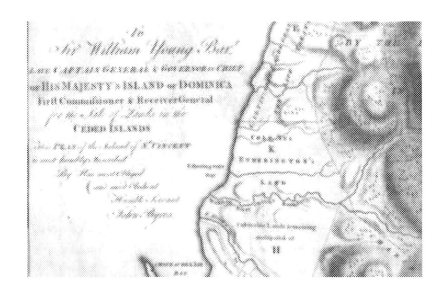

Detail view of Byre's 1776 St. Vincent map showing Etherington's land grant.

Photo of same, used with permission of the William L. Clements Library, University of Michigan.

consisting of 100 to 200 men.[86] Governor Morris expressed his displeasure at the replacements, whom he described as "useless...sent even without Arms." This was further fueled by his dispute with the St. Vincent's Assembly over the granting of funds to pay the local militia, which they felt was the responsibility of Great Britain.

This issue regarding troops was a significant one. The Caribbean colonies had traditionally been willing to support troops not only to defend against foreign invasion but also against slave and maroon (as well as Carib) revolts.[87] In addition, the colony governments had favored regular British troops over indigenous ones, due to the difficulties in maintaining local militia, which included traveling distances, proper military training and again, cost.[88] St. Vincent's was no exception with regard to these aspects. The loss of the King's troops left the island more vulnerable in the event of an attack, but also to internal conflicts that were to arise.

A tangential addition to this was the conflict that developed between the Carib and slave populations at St. Vincent's. Regular troops had been utilized in the various Caribbean islands to put down multiple slave revolts that had occurred during the past decade, notably at Jamaica, Tobago, and Montserrat (as well as the previously detailed 1773 war with the Caribs at St. Vincent's).[89] Despite the French influence on the Caribs against the British, it is somewhat ironic that both groups incited the Caribs and Negro slaves against each other, and used the Caribs as "pawns" for their own purposes. At St. Vincent's, an escalation in Caribs sheltering runaway slaves (the latter who held the British responsible for the food and supply shortages), as well as raids conducted on plantations for kidnapping of slaves, caused alarm among the plantation owners and government officials that led Governor Morris to mobilize militia to deal with these various incidents in 1777.[90] Not only did this result in an increased cost for rewards for returned slaves but the payment of the militia troops as well. As previously discussed, this was in essence a two-fold problem. The plantation owners and the Assembly were less in favor of using militia forces for this, in part, since the enforcement entailed their own involvement. However, despite their preference for the utilization of the island's regular troops for these purposes, they were reluctant to cover the increase in cost for all of this, hence the continuing dispute between the governor over the militia act and expenses in running the island government. Despite these problems, the troops that did remain at St. Vincent's were on the alert for the threat of

French attack, in addition to internal disturbances as they might arise.

With regard to the defense against outside invasion, there were numerous other problems that compounded even further those just described. Despite the various West Indies colonial governments insistence for regular British troops for defense against slave and native revolts, their presence was only envisioned as a supportive measure. The Royal Navy was considered as the most effective deterrent against "foreign" invasion.[91] Similar to the problems faced by the British Army (and the 60th Royal American Regiment in particular) in North America during the 1763 Indian Uprising, small garrisons and isolated forts were most inadequate to account for any meaningful defense, and once again, St. Vincent's was no exception to this.

Nonetheless, being responsible for the island's protection and military preparedness, Governor Morris took what measures he could, although as it has been discussed so far, he was the cause of some of his own various difficulties. The problem in lack of supplies was again at the forefront. A perfect example of this is when, on 9 February 1777 at St. Vincent's, Governor Morris commandeered military supplies from the "store ship" *Nottingham*, which had been designated for Tobago, since nothing he had requested two years ago was on board, save for "a fire engine and some ammunition."[92] This seizure netted "117 six-pound shot, five boxes of tin-case shot, a bundle of match, and three wad-hooks and rammers" which helped somewhat. Yet by late August, Governor Morris implored Lord Germain, the powerful British Secretary of State for the American Department, for further subsistence of "proper Stores and Ordnance" due to increasing chance of an "impending attack" on the Island.[93]

Of interesting note is that the population of St. Vincent's at this time totaled "911 men, 126 women, and 1,810 children with 5,500 Caribs, 1,200 runaway Negroes, and 10,391 slaves."[94] This compared to a population of "2397 Whites, 1050 free Negroes, and 10,752 slaves" at the nearby Island of St. Lucia (with Tobago's total population estimated to be this as well).[95]

In October, **Duncan Campbell**, later to appear as a prosecution witness in the court-martial, and William Crooke, both Assembly members, conspired to forge certain documents in order to implicate Governor Morris in an issue of "personal land-grants." In fact, the Governor did make grants to the benefit of his family and on his own behalf, thereby violating his own aforementioned policies. Morris's grants to himself were held, "in trust," by **Doctor Robert Glasgow,**[96] soon to appear as a prosecution witness in the court-martial. These controversial land issues were an underlying vital part in the court-martial disputes and were, as previously noted, to involve Etherington to a large degree. Some comment has already been made concerning his land grant from the Caribs as a result of his actions in the 1773 treaty negotiations and the later "completion" of that transaction, whatever that may be. However, again, exact details are lacking as to how and why this truly came about; again, additional comment will be discussed in Part III of the trial proceedings analysis.

Nonetheless, it is clear that Etherington continued on good terms with the Caribs as is evident by his subsequent appointment as military commander at St. Vincent's. With tensions on the island fragile due to the perceived threat of another Carib war resulting from the land controversy and their hiding of runaway slaves (the Caribs were slave owners themselves ironically as earlier noted). To help maintain the peace, on 31 October, Lord George Germain informed the governor that he was *sending* **Lieutenant Colonel Etherington** " to be in charge of the Caribs over whom I understand he has considerable influence, having gained their confidence, by a humane attention to their complaints, and a strict regard to justice and good faith."[97]

(Apparently Etherington was *on the Island* in October when Lord Germain said he was *sending* him, and he was, at that time, in charge of the 60th Regiment, as an exchange of letters between Captain Robert Morse, Commanding Engineer in the Ceded Islands, and Senior Officer, and Lord William Barrington, Secretary at War, the documents dated 26 May 1777 and 11 August 1777, respectively, indicate. Therefore, the reference to *sending* may have better put as *ordering*.)[98]

Fortunately, no Carib hostilities erupted as the civil government and the military were able to keep peace, although tenuous, through political means.

1778

By early March, France signed a treaty of alliance and officially joined the American cause in the Revolutionary War. An interesting sidelight in this alliance was the United States' agreement to cede any captured Caribbean islands to France.[99] As a result, the concern for potential invasion by either the French or Spanish (the latter of whom had also become an ally of the Americans) was even more escalated and added further tension. When the French admiral, Monsignor Le Compte D'Estaing, sailed from Toulon for the Caribbean in April, the British government sent a "confidential" notice to the colonial governors directing them "to prepare in any way possible."[100]

By June, the status of relations between the plantation owners and the civil government at St. Vincent's was non-salvageable. Governor Morris did have good intentions with regard to the improvement and overall well-being of the island, and, in fact, spent considerable sums of his own money towards that end. Like their counterparts in the American colonies, the governor and plantation owners each had their own ideas and agendas as to the actual course and management of these aspects. Although thanked by the Assembly for these efforts, they declined, however, to reimburse him.[101] The tumultuous course of the last four years which had included the disagreements over the development plan, duty taxes for the governor's salary, management of the Carib and slave problems, and controversy over the land grants all resulted in numerous complaints, charges and counter-charges between Morris and the Assembly being forwarded to Lord Germain back in England.

This crescendoed by late 1778 with the dissolution of the Assembly by Morris, and a dispute over having no official militia to assist in the defense of the colony since the local militia act had recently again expired. The latter was a most important contributing factor to the ensuing events that resulted in the surrender of St. Vincent's the following year. The summary and final understanding of all this is that the power struggle was essentially the same as that in the American colonies in a general principle; that being the Colonial Assemblies attempting to exercise their perceived rights "in fear of the prerogative...and potential exorbitant powers of the Governors" i.e., Colonial rights versus Imperial powers, as one historian has defined it.[102] Despite the threat of invasion of the Caribbean being imminent, the British government was indecisive as to just how it wanted to manage both the American and the West Indies corridors, which resulted in Dominica being the first of their Caribbean islands to fall on 7 September 1778.

1779

At St. Vincent's, at the time of the surrender of Dominica, the internal "political bickering" continued between the inhabitants and

Governor Morris. This subsequently added to the "military unpreparedness" of the island, which provided an easy avenue for the French invasion. On Martinique, Admiral Compte D'Estaing and Governor Marquis De Bouille drew up their plans.[103] On St. Vincent's, the Caribs upon learning that France had declared war on the English, immediately invited the French to send spies to inspect the weakness of the colony in order to "*concert* a plan for its destruction." This was not surprising since the Caribs had never fully accepted the terms of the 1773 treaty with the British, although it was somewhat ironic, since the French, like the British, had attempted to exterminate the Caribs during early settlement in the Caribbean. In any event, one of the French emissaries, Percin La Rocque Venturin (Monsignor Du Perier La Rocque) was captured and brought in for questioning by Governor Morris before being confined in "gaol." Shortly thereafter, however, he escaped and returned to Martinique having been assured by the Caribs of their support.[104] Having secured the assistance of their allies, the French immediately began to land arms, ammunition, and other supplies at Grand Sable, on the Windward Side near the principle Carib outpost of the island (the latter being Bayabou[105]).

Mons. Gelfrier, a French planter, gave "intelligence" to Governor Morris regarding the French being amongst the Caribs. Upon learning of this, Morris ordered a party to Grand Sable to ascertain the fact of the matter and the 'cool reception' they received betrayed their intentions.

In early 1779, Lieutenant Colonel Etherington returned from recruiting for the Royal Americans in Europe "with a number of raw recruits from England."[106] Subsequently, he *allegedly* employed most of the troops clearing timber on his aforementioned land grant he had been allotted by the Carib chief, Chatoyer, while leaving token forces at the small posts and settlements along the coast. This alleged action is of utmost importance in the dispute between Etherington and Morris as will be seen in the course of the trial. Apparently, the French were aware of these troop disbursements and this was taken into account regarding their invasion plans.

In the period of the 10th to 15th June, Admiral D'Estaing sent out the St. Vincent's invasion force under the command of Mons. Le Chevalier Du Rumain. This expedition included four captured English vessels, "the frigates *Lively* and *Ellis*, the corvette *Weazle*, and the brig *Reprisal*, together with a French schooner, the *Marie-Catherine*" and troops on board from "the Regiment de Champagne, the Grenadiers de Viennois, and the Regiment de la Martinique, two detachments of Militia, and some Marines."[107] Initially, heavy

British Private, 60th or Royal American Regiment of Foot, ca. 1772-81. Although originally drawn to depict the uniform of the King's 8th Regiment, nonetheless, the uniform shown is the standard British infantryman's dress of the Revolutionary period and would have been exactly the same for the 60th Regiment troops at St. Vincent from 1773 to 1779. Being a Royal Regiment, the facings were of dark blue, turnbacks on the coats were white as was the waistcoat. Illustration by Dirk Gringhuis, published with permission, Courtesy: Mackinac State Historic Parks.

weather and adverse winds were encountered and the expedition was forced back to Martinique. On the 15th, however, Du Rumain was able to land a contingent of forty-five men at a site (probably Byrea Beach) just south of the original planned landing at Grand Sable due to "rough seas." Upon landing, the French ranks were immediately swelled by about 600 Caribs, according to some estimates.

On the next morning, a blatant mistake by some of the island's defenders essentially sealed St. Vincent's fate. Three of the French ships appeared off Calliaqua (one of the small coastal settlements and posts) and anchored in Young's Bay, "about nine o'clock in the morning...without "shewing any colours."[108] Unfortunately, despite vehement protests by one of the artillery gunners of the Hyde's Point Battery at the entrance to the bay who suspected them to be enemy ships, they were not fired upon since the plantation owners mistakenly thought them to be the "expected merchant ships from Antigua." This costly mistake enabled the invading force to rendezvous with the previously landed force and thus proceed with virtual ease along the coast towards Kingstown.

At Fort Colonaire (Colonaire), one of the posts with a small contingent of 60th troops and armed plantation owners, a valiant stand was made under the direction the commanding officer Lieutenant David Gordon and Mr. James Glasgow, "until being overpowered by superior numbers" of the initial landing force. The combined French-Carib force then immediately embarked on a campaign of "the most flagrant acts of insolence and cruelty; plunder, violence, and murder..." against the coastal settlements and eventually meeting up with their counterparts for the assault on Kingstown.[109] In the meantime, Governor Morris and the few inhabitants at Zion Hill (Sion or Mr. Hartley's Hill, just outside Kingstown), which the governor had "proposed to defend with two pieces of ordinance, until the arrival of the troops," frantically erected temporary defense works. Lieutenant Colonel Etherington was by this time aware of hostilities, and had managed to join the Governor with an advanced detachment of 60th troops.

At this point, the people and events, *set on a collision course in* 1763, finally converge — resulting in the surrender of St. Vincent's to the French and eventually the **Court-Martial of Colonel George Etherington.** Following the surrender, Governor Morris was furious and spent the next year seeking and eventually obtaining a Court of Inquiry against Etherington in late 1780. Having remained eight months at St. Vincent's, which had been granted to him and other government officials by the French to complete personal business

British (Private Enlisted Men's) Pewter Military Buttons of the 60th or Royal American Regiment, ca. 1768-1776, and ca. 1776-1790.

The original button shown with only the numerical "60th" would have been the type worn by the 60th Regiment troops garrisoned at St. Vincent's Island from 1773-1776. Thereafter, including to 1779 at St. Vincent's, a variation of the button was adapted for the regiment which included a floral wreath border surrounding a smaller numerical "60th" of the same Arabic motif as shown here by the adjacent button. Photo of the earlier pattern original button by: Co-author Todd Harburn, published with permission, Courtesy: Mackinac State Historic Parks; photo of later pattern original button, published with permission, Courtesy, "Don Troiani Collection."

affairs, he returned to Antigua in February 1780. After much difficulty through multiple requests to Lord George Germain and the British military, he was finally granted the inquiry into his conduct and that of Lieutenant Colonel Etherington. The Court, consisting of Lieutenant General Thomas Gage, Major General William Tryon, and Major General Edward Matthew suggested that the governor would "...have been inclined to resist, with spirit, the attack of the enemy on 16 June, 1779, if he had been well advised and properly supported," and that Etherington had "lacked zeal," afterward ordering that he stand trial.[110] The details of the subsequent court-martial will be extensively brought out in the progress of its transcript, and, as presented in the next section, finally reveals the *real* truth about this intriguing event.

♔ PART II

PROCEEDINGS OF A GENERAL COURT-MARTIAL HELD ON THE ISLAND OF ST. LUCIA IN THE WEST INDIES, THE FIFTH DAY OF OCTOBER 1781

Charges brought by Valentine Morris, Esq., late Governor of the Island of St. Vincent's, against Lieutenant Colonel George Etherington, of the 2nd Battalion, 60th or Royal American Regiment of Foot.

Before presenting the trial transcript in its entirety, a few preliminary comments are both appropriate and helpful to the reader. First, according to Governor Morris's account, there were 20 posts in existence on the island at the time of the French invasion, as follows:[111]

Oya Rabacca	Temporary Station at Stubb's Estate
La Colonarie	Battery at Wilkin's Point (at the Grand View Hotel)
Byrea Redoubt	Point Calliaqua Barracks/Millington's Point
Government House	Hyde's Point (now Rathos Mill – Cane Garden)
The Guard House	Old Woman's Point
Kingstown Barracks	Morris's Battery (over the Town – Dorchester Hill)
Bayabou	Barrouli or Queen's Bay
Layou Town Battery	Layou Outward Point Battery
Chateaubellair Barracks	*A Post on **Etherington's** Land (Walibou – Round Top Hill)
Doyle's Battery	The Ordnance Battery in Kingstown

As previously noted, this is a key factor in the allegations against Etherington and the subsequent importance will be apparent at the conclusion of the trial proceedings.

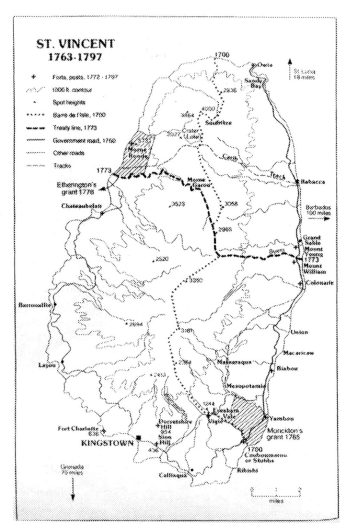

Map of St. Vincent showing location of the twenty posts existing in 1779.
Reprinted from Michael Craton: *Testing the Chains: Resistance to Slavery in the British West Indies.* Copyright ©1982, Cornell University Press. Used by permission of the publisher, Cornell University Press.

Secondly, the biographical sketches of the principle participants, **Lieutenant Colonel George Etherington**, **Governor Valentine Morris, Esq.**, and **Chatoyer**, have already been presented. However, the following names comprise the list of witnesses who presented testimony in the trial. A brief comment is included regarding identification of these individuals, which should be helpful to the reader in distinguishing "who's who" during the course of the proceedings.

Prosecution Witness List (with comments)

Richard Rellan – Late Assistant Mate of the Hospital at St. Vincent's. *(Note: From his testimony it is quite apparent that he is an avid Morris supporter.)*

Duncan Campbell – Planter. *(Note: While not necessarily an Etherington supporter, he definitely is anti-Morris. He and William Crooke had at one time joined in a conspiracy to use forged documents in order to raise an issue, in Assembly, of Morris's personal land grants, made to himself and his family as well.)*

Mr. William Richardson – Carpenter. *(Note: His testimony, what little of it there is, does seem to favor Governor Morris at Etherington's expense.)*

Doctor John Connor – Physician. *(Note: The doctor is perhaps best thought of as an Etherington detractor rather than, necessarily, a Morris supporter; however, the testimony he offers is often crafted in such a way as to support Morris's position at Etherington's expense.)*

Doctor Robert Glasgow – Physician. *(Note: Doctor Glasgow must be a very close friend of the governor's as his testimony indicates; in addition, it was he that held Morris's land grants to himself, in trust.)*

Mr. George Bolton – Shopkeeper in St. Vincent's. *(Note: He seems to be a Morris supporter although he offered little testimony with insignificant impact.)*

Doctor Patrick Connor – Physician. *(Note: Doctor Patrick Connor seems to be quite neutral, however, the abundance of his testimony was in support of the colonel.)*

Mr. George Fraser – Deputy Commissary. *(Note: He offered little in the way of testimony and seemed to be quite neutral as if not wanting to offend either party.)*

Mr. Henry Wilkie – Unstated occupation. *(Note: He was a close friend of John Byres, the Crown Surveyor, who, in turn, was a close friend of Etherington as evidenced by the fact that his 1776 Map of Bequia was dedicated to the colonel. The little testimony offered had no impact whatsoever.)*

Captain William Kelly[112] – of His Majesty's 60th Regiment. *(Note: His testimony, while detailed and apparently factual, did much to support Etherington.)*

Ensign Hubert Van Hamel – of His Majesty's 60th Regiment. *(Note: His testimony, while seemingly factual and quite detailed did much to support Etherington.)*

Sergeant Major John Ayres – of His Majesty's 60th Regiment. *(Note: His testimony, while seemingly factual and quite detailed, did much to support Etherington.)*

Sergeant John McMullan – of His Majesty's 60th Regiment. *(Note: His testimony was very limited, but what little there was, supported Etherington.)*

Defense Witness List *(with comments)*

Doctor George Young – late of the Military Hospital in St. Vincent's, first Curator of the Botanic Garden in St. Vincent's, late Member of the Council in St. Vincent's. *(Note: His testimony was quite neutral but of great significance to Etherington's cause.)*

It is important to note the following aspects as well. Morris had been adamant in his requests that the trial be held in the West Indies and not England, so that "all the Witnesses would be willing to attend...and information not suppressed or wanting."[113] Ironically, however, (and perhaps even more exasperating to Morris himself), he was not even able to attend due to being detained by a creditor from one of his bills on the island's treasury during his tenure.

Finally, from this point forward, the narrative will take on three parts: the presentation of the original trial transcript proceedings; a

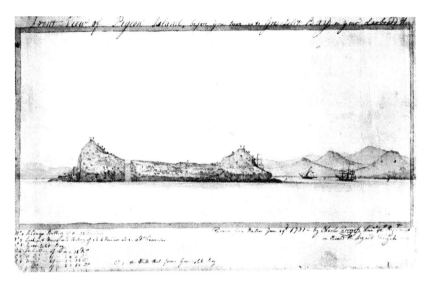

"Front View of Pigeon Island
...Drawn from Nature June 29th 1781, by Lieutenant Charles Forrest."

Here were massive British fortifications with many buildings, the ruins of which are maintained at St. Lucia today. Drawn just three months before the Etherington trial began, this sketch again provides some fine detail and particularly the British ships in the bay similar to the other sketches made by Forrest. Original sketch in the collections of the William L. Clements Library. Photo of same, used with permission, Courtesy of: William L. Clements Library, University of Michigan.

presentation of the *'FACTS'* as they were traditionally offered along with Etherington's defense pleadings; and the Evidences given in testimony by the fourteen witnesses. The traditional presentation is preceded by, **"Morris,"** Etherington's comments, by **"Etherington,"** and Witness testimony by indicating the source. Where appropriate, "comments" will be italicized, and indicated by the term "*Note.*"

Thus, the following account is the previously unpublished official transcript of George Etherington's court-martial trial, which is reprinted here with the kind permission of the Public Record Office in Kew, England.[114] In order to present the text in the manner of the day, care has been taken to retain the original spelling and grammar as much as possible, with exceptions made for clarity and ease of reading.

THE ETHERINGTON COURT-MARTIAL TRANSCRIPT

1781 HELD AT ST. LUCIA

At a General Court-martial held on the Island of St. Lucia In the West Indies the fifth day of October 1781, by Virtue of a Warrant from Gabriel Christie, Esq. Brigadier General Commanding His Majesty's Forces in the Leeward and Charibbe Islands, &c., &c., &c. directed to Major William Chester of His Majesty's 35th Regiment and bearing the date of the 29th day of September 1781.

Present

Major William Chester of the 35th Regiment, President

Captain Hunt Fitzgerrald-35th Regt.	**M**	Captain Hugh Massy-35th. Regt.
Captn. Humphry May-46th	**e**	Captn. George Mathews-46th
Captn. Bryan Bill-46th	**m**	Captain Richard Norris-27th
Captn. William Hewetson-46th	**b**	Captn. Thomas Williams-35th
Captn. Ebenezer Vavasov-27th	**e**	Captn. William Evans-87th
Captn. James Boys-87th	**r**	Captn. Fitz Maurice Caldwell-86th
	s	

Captain Cornelius Smelt 35th Regiment Deputy Judge Advocate

The Court being duly constituted and sworn

At a General Court Martial

held on the Island of St. Lucia in the West Indies the fifth day of
October 1781, by Virtue of a Warrant from Gabriel Christie Esqr. Brigadier
General Commanding His Majesty's Forces in the Leeward and Charible
Islands &c. &c. &c. directed to Major William Chester of His Majesty's
35th. Regiment and bearing date the 29th. day of September 1781.

Present

Major William Chester of the 35th. Regiment President

Captain Hunt FitzGerald 35th. Regt.	Captain Hugh Massey 35th. Regt.
Captn. Humphry May 46th.	Capt. George Matthews 46th.
Capt. Bryan Bell 46th.	Captain Richard Norris 27th.
Capt. William Hewetson 46th.	Capt. Thomas Williams 35th.
Capt. Ebenezer Vavasor 27th.	Captn. William Evans 87th.
Capt. James Boys 87th.	Capt. Fitz Maurice Caldwell 86th.

Members

Captain Cornelius Sonett 35th. Regiment Deputy Judge Advocate

The Court being duly constituted and sworn

Lieutenant Colo. George Etherington

of the 2d. Battalion of the 60th. or Royal American Regiment of Foot
was brought before it on a complaint exhibited against him by Valli
Morris Esqr. late Governor of the Island of St. Vincents, whereby the
said Lieutenant Colonel George Etherington is charged with Giving in

First Charge False Returns and;

Second Charge Improperly employing some of the Forces then under his
Command, in cutting down Wood and doing other Works upon
his own Estate and for his own private benefit in the said

Island

**First page of the
1781 Etherington General Court Martial transcript.**

Photocopy of original, published with permission, Courtesy: Public
Record Office, Kew, Surrey, England (PRO/WO 71/58, ff 271-337).

Lieutenant Colo. George Etherington of the 2nd Battalion of the 60th or Royal American Regiment of Foot, was brought before it on a complaint exhibited Against him by Vall; Morris Esq. late Governor of the Island of St. Vincent's, Whereby the

(First Charge) said Lieutenant Colonel George Etherington is charged with Giving in False Returns and;

(Second Charge) Improperly employing some of the Forces then under his... Command, in cutting down Wood and doing other Works upon — his own Estate and for his own private benefit in the said Island of St. Vincent's; and also with

(Third Charge) Disobeying several Orders given by the said Governor respecting the Distribution of Troops for the safety and defence of the said — Island particularly Orders given on the 17th day of September, 7th, day of October and 19th day of December 1778 and on the 1st day of April and 16th day of June 1779; and furthermore with

(Fourth Charge) Neglect of duty and with improper behaviour in the Face of the Enemy; and also,

(Fifth Charge) After the Capture of the said Island by advising, and endeavoring to induce the Governor to admit of alterations and — additions in the Articles of Capitulation more advantageous to the Enemy and Derogatory to His Majesty's Honor and Dignity.

The Deputy Judge Advocate represented to the Court, that from the short notice he had been able to give the Public, of the present Trial, some of the Witnesses capable of — giving material Testimony touching the Charges exhibited against the Prisoner, had not time to appear, in consequence of which, the President adjourned the Court until to morrow Morning at ten o'clock.

Saturday 6th October 1781

Prosecution

Evidence

Mr. Richard Rellan late an assistant Mate of the Hospital at St. Vincent's having been duly sworn was examined as to the

<u>1st Charge</u>   <u>Giving in false Returns</u>

Q. by the court — What do you know as to this charge.
A. I know nothing of it.

Being examined as to the

<u>2nd Charge</u>   <u>Improperly employing some of the Forces &c. &c. &c.</u>

Q. by the Court — Do you know that there were any Men · employed on the Prisoner's Estate when the French — landed.
A. There were Men there but I do not know what Work they were employed in.

Q. Do you know <u>for certain</u> that there were any Men employ'd cutting Wood on the Prisoner's Estate.
A. I have been told so by the Soldiers — <u>themselves</u> who were employ'd at his Estate, whom I have often seen going there and returning from it.

Q. What number of Soldiers have you seen going to and from his Estate.
A. I have seen sometimes eight and sometimes ten.

Q. Did you see any Soldiers come from the Prisoner's Estate after the Island was surrendered.
A. I saw the Troops march in, from the — Prisoner's Estate and some said they came from the Prisoner's Land.

Q. Were those who said they came from — Prisoner's Land Cloathed as Soldiers of the 60th Regiment and Armed and Accoutred as Soldiers shou'd be on such an occasion.
A. Some of them were Armed and Cloathed — properly and some were not.

Q. From what Post did the Soldiers come whom you have seen going to Work on the Prisoner's Land.
A. From Princes Town where the Barracks were.

The Evidence being examined as to the

3rd Charge
 Disobeying several Orders given by the said Governor &c. &c. &c.

Q. by the Court — Do you know if the Prisoner ever disobey'd
any Orders given out on the 17th September, 7th October, 16th
December 1778 and on the 1st April & 16th June 1779.
 A. No, except on the 16th of June 1779.

Q. In what particulars did the Prisoner disobey Governor
Morris's Orders on the 16th June 1779.
 A. I heard Governor Morris say /in Company/ that he had
ordered the Prisoner to March from the — Barracks to Mr. Hartley's
Hill, and that it was two Hours before he arrived there.

Q. How long after the Capitulation was it that you heard
Governor Morris say so.
 A. Two or three days.

The Evidence being examined as to the

4th Charge
 Neglect of duty and improper behaviour &c. &c.

Deposed that on the 16th June 1779 /which was the day the
— French landed at St. Vincent's/ he was in the Fort above
the Town of Kingstown; That Governor Morris Captain
Cunningham and Mr. Lees the Engineer were there, and had
pointed an Eighteen Pounder at the Enemy who were on their
March to the Fort. That Governor Morris directed Captain
Cunningham who had a lighted Match in his hand, to fire the
Gun at the Enemy if they advanced further; That the —
Prisoner thereupon told the Governor that it was more than
they durst do, and addressing himself particularly to Mr. Lees,
ask'd, "If he ever heard of a Gun being fired at an Enemy,
after a Flag of Truce had been sent to them? and which was
not return'd; That Mr. Lees — answer'd he knew nothing
about it; The Deponent being then order'd away from the
Fort, knows not what passed there afterwards.

The Deponent further says that about three days after the Island was surrendered to the French he heard very high Words pass between the Prisoner and Governor Morris respecting the signing of some Papers, the contents of which he is ignorant of, but — was informed by Governor Morris's Clerk, that these Papers were — concerning the distribution of the Troops at St. Vincent's prior to the landing of the Enemy. The Deponent produced to the Court a return of a Detachment of the British Troops at Fort Guilford dated 14th April 1779 which consisted of 2 Subs 2 Serjeants 2 Drummers and 20 Rank and File which he declares was more than was at any other Post, in the Charibbe Country, and that there was no addition made afterwards.

Q. by the Court — Was the distribution of the Troops at St. Vincent's agreeable to Governor Morris's Orders.
A. I have often heard Governor Morris complain that it was not.

Q. How many British Troops were in the Fort when the French advanced towards it.
A. I counted forty two.

Q. How many British Troops were there on the Island at the time it was attack'd.
A. Above Two hundred.

Q. Did you ever hear any reason assign'd for there being so few Men in the Fort at the time the French attack'd the Island.
A. I have.

Q. What was it.
A. I heard there were from 60 to 70 Men employ'd cutting down Wood on the Prisoner's Estate.

Q. How many of the Enemy's Troops landed on the Island.
A. To the best of my Judgement there were Three hundred and fifty.

Q. How many Men were under Arms for the — defence of the Island when it was attack'd.
A. At the Post where I was, there were forty two, but I know not how the rest were disposed of.

Q. Were those properly dressed and appointed that were at the Post you was at?

A. I cannot say.

Q. Do you think that the Troops at the Post you were, were in a situation of making a stand against the Enemy?

A. It is my opinion they were able to drive the Enemy off the island.

Q. Was there any action between the Troops at the Post where you were and the French?

A. There was not a Gun fired.

Q. Did the Prisoner appear anxious to Engage the Enemy?

A. He did not.

Q. What are your reasons for saying so?

A. He appear'd to be in great confusion.

Court — Explain yourself.

A. On the Prisoner's return from — the Commander of the French Troops he told Governor Morris that Articles of Capitulation were agreed upon, and the Fort and Out Posts should be given up by four o'clock; upon which Governor Morris took out his Watch and said that it was then half past two — o'clock and therefore impossible — The Prisoner answered that — the Fort must be delivered up at that time — The Governor — declared he would not give it up until the Capitulation was signed, upon which the Prisoner said that if it was not, the Enemy would March in and cut their Throats; Thereupon many of the principal Gentlemen of the Island struck their Firelocks against the Ground being much vexed at the Prisoner's expression.

Q. Was the Prisoner sent by Governor — Morris more than once to treat with the Enemy about a Capitulation?

A. I think he was sent twice.

Q. Did the Governor or the Prisoner propose a Capitulation first.

A. I don't know.

Q. Did the Prisoner on his return to the Fort, use any other expressions than those you already related, to induce Governor Morris to surrender the Fort without making a — Defence.

A. I did not hear any.

Q. Had you any notice of the Enemy's arrival before they landed?

A. I heard Governor Morris say that he had notice four or five days before.

Q. In consequence of that information were the Out Posts called in and proper steps taken to defend the Island?

A. Governor Morris said, that two or three days before he had sent for the Prisoner, and had mentioned to him that the Men were not come in from his Estate, and that he expected the French to land every hour, and the Prisoner in reply told the Governor not to be uneasy as the Men would be up time enough.

Q. On the day the French landed did you hear — the Governor say how the Troops were employed?

A. I did not.

Q. Who was the officer sent to the Enemy — first with a Flag of Truce?

A. Ensign Van Hamel of the 60th.

Q. What was the business he was sent on.

A. I heard the Prisoner tell him to ask the Enemy what was the business they came about and what they wanted.

Q. What answer was brought back.

A. I do not know for I did not see him again 'till after the Island was surrendered.

Q. From the time the Enemy landed how long was it before they advanced to the Works.

A. I believe it was two hours after.

Q. How far was it from the Prisoner's Estate to the Post where you were?

A. Twenty Miles

Q. Did the Enemy land any Cannon?

A. I never heard they did.

Q. Did you ever hear any officers of the 60th Regiment, who were in the Fort on that day, give their — opinions of the Prisoners behaviour?
A. No I did not.

Q. Did the Prisoner on that day support the Character of a British Officer and the Honor of the British Army in your Opinion?
A. I don't think he did.

Q. Was there time enough for all the — Troops or any part of them to have joined the Prisoner from the — time the Alarm was given to the time the Enemy landed.
A. There was no alarm untill the Enemy landed.

Q. Did you ever hear Governor Morris censure the Prisoner's Conduct when the Prisoner was present.
A. I never did.

Q. Does the Ground from the place where the Enemy landed to the Works, afford any situations, where the Prisoner might have engaged the Enemy to advantage, with the — Force he had?
A. Yes.

Q. Did the Governor seem anxious to Engage the Enemy?
A. He did.

Q. With what number of Troops including the Militia cou'd the Prisoner have attack'd the Enemy?
A. Eighty two.

Q. Did the Troops and Militia seem anxious to try their strength with the Enemy?
A. The Militia seem'd very anxious, and the King's Troops wou'd have done their duty had they been ordered.

Q. Who prevented them!
A. The Prisoner wou'd not allow the Gun to be fired, and I believe that was the reason.

Q. What was the Enemy's force composed of?

A. Some were Regulars, some Volunteers, composed of white people, Negroes and Mulattoes.

Q. Did you ever hear what number of Regulars they had?
A. I did not.

Q. Did the Troops retreat from the Fort, on the advance of the Enemy?
A. They did not.

Q. When did the Enemy take possession of the Fort?
A. The day after.

Q. Was the Capitulation signed before the Enemy took possession of the Fort?
A. Yes.

Q. Could not the Troops have retired and joined those in the Country?
A. Yes.

Q. Was the Fort tenable until the Troops in the Country cou'd have joined you?
A. Yes.

Q. Could the Enemy have taken a position to prevent a junction of your force?
A. They could not prevent a junction, except with those in the Charibbe Country.

Q. How soon could the whole force of the Island have been collected?
A. The Troops from the Charibbe Country cou'd not have joined, but those from the other Posts might in eight Hours.

Q. How many were in the Charibbe Country?
A. Upwards of one hundred.

Q. Was not the position taken by the French Troops such, as to cut off the Communication of the detached Posts with the Fort, without bringing on an action?
A. The Troops to Leeward could have joined without engaging the Enemy.

Q. Were any Charibbs in Arms to assist the — Enemy?

A. I heard there were Charibbs in — Arms, but know not the part they would have taken.

Q. Could the Troops posted at Chatteaubellair have joined?

A. I think they could.

Q. Who Commanded the Troops at — Chatteaubellair?

A. Captain Kelly of the 60th Regiment.

Q. How far distant is Chatteaubellair — from the Fort?

A. Sixteen or seventeen Miles.

Q. In what time cou'd the Troop there have marched to the Fort?

A. In six hours.

Q. What is the distance of Princestown from the Fort?

A. Eleven Miles.

Q. Was any of the Troops quartered at Princes Town under arms at the Fort the 16th June 1779?

A. No.

Q. How many Men were quartered at Princes Town?

A. I don't know.

Q. In what time might the detachment at Princes Town have march'd to the Fort?

A. In about two hours and a half.

Q. Did you ever hear any of the Officers of the 60th Regiment speak of the Surrender of the Island?

A. I have.

Q. Who were they?

A. I heard Wm. Charlton and another Officer say that they had been in the Army many Years and had never seen so shameful and dirty an affair, or Words to that purpose.

Q. Who were the Officers of the 60th Regt. that were in the Fort that day?

A. Captain Etherington Wm. Wheatly, Wm. Charlton Lieutenant Walker and Lieutenant Barker.

The Evidence being examined as

5th Charge
Also after the Capture of the said Island &c.&c.&c

Q. by the Court — Did you ever hear that the — Prisoner advised the Governor to alter the Articles of Capitulation in favour of the Enemy?
A. I never did.

Q. by the Prisoner — Did you hear the Governor order me to send for the Troops?
A. A. I did not.

Q. Was not the Flag of Truce out when you say I prevented the Gun to be fired?
A. It was.

The Court adjourned to meet on Monday
Morning at Ten o'clock

Monday 8th October 1781

The Court met according to adjournment.

Evidence
Mr. Duncan Campbell Planter
at St. Vincent's when the Island was attack'd /having been duly sworn/ was examined as to the

1st Charge   Giving in false Returns

Answ. I know nothing relative to this Charge.
The Evidence being examined as to the

2nd Charge
Improperly employing some of the Forces &c. &c. &c.

Ans. I saw Soldiers of the 60th Regiment in the Month of March or April 1779 cutting down Wood upon the — Prisoner's Land at Morn Garow.

Q. by the Court — Do you know — whether it was for his own private benefit?
A. I believe so.

Q. What number of Soldiers did you see so employed?
A. Above Ten.

Q. Were there any Public Works going on at the place, where you saw the Soldiers of the 60th Regiment at Work?
A. None that I know of.

Q. Was the Ground they were working on, likely to have Public Works erected upon it?
A. No.

Q. The Men you saw employed, were they carrying Materials proper to form public Works?
A. They were employed burning and — clearing the Ground.

Q. Did you ever hear Governor Morris find fault with the Prisoner for employing the Soldiers of the 60th Regiment upon his Estate?
A. I never did.

The Evidence being examined as to the

3rd Charge
Disobeying several Orders &c. &c. &c.

Q. by the court — Do you know any instances of the Prisoner's disobedience of Orders on the days specified in the Charge?
A. No.
The Evidence being examined as to the

4th Charge
Neglect of duty and improper behaviour &c. &c. &c.
Answ. On the Morning of the 16th June 1779 when the Enemy landed, I set out with Mr. Geo: Fraser on Horsback, and we rode to a point of Land on which there was a Battery of three — Guns, and opposite to which, the Enemy's Ships lay. I told Mr. Fraser that I

was afraid the Island wou'd be taken without the firing of a Gun, upon which he reply'd they shall not have that to say, for we will fire the few Guns that are at the Battery. We went to the Battery, and found the Guns unloaded, upon which we went and broke the door of the Governor's House, but cou'd not find any Cartridges or Powder, whilst we were in the House a Negroe came in and told us, that there were a party of the French Marching towards the Battery, upon which we run out, and mounted our Horses, and were obliged to go down a precipice to the Sea; as the Enemy had got between us and the main Road; We made our escape, and went towards the Town; We saw Mr. Lees the Engineer at the Intrenchments on the top of Hartley's Hill with a few Negroes, we rode up to him and asked him if Governor Morris and Colonel Etherington were making any preparations to repell the Enemy, he said they were not, nor did he believe they meant to make any, -- he said he had been sent there by the Governor, who told him that he wou'd meet the King's Troops there, but that he cou'd not as yet observe them in motion, we then left him, and went to Town, where we met Doctor John Connor, who went on with us towards the Government House, Doctor Connor said, "do you go into the Governor and hurry him, and I will ride up to the Barracks to see what keeps Colonel Etherington," I went in to the Governor who I found surrounded with Women and a Mr. Malloun and some others, I address'd myself to the Governor and said, I suppose you are informed that the Enemy have landed, and are now on their march — towards the Town; He said he knew of their intentions of taking the Island some days ago, -- I answered, as that was the case, why was he not — more forward in his preparations to receive them; At this time Mr. — Malloun, who was a person in the confidence of the Governor, took me aside, and said, that he had been preparing something in the form of a Capitulation, which he had chiefly taken from the Dominica one, which he had then in his Pocket; He desired me to look over what he had wrote. I told him that it wou'd be time enough when it was determined to give up the Island; I then went to the Governor who was in the front Gallery, and ask'd if he meant to make any Defence — he said, "he did, a most desperate one," I then ask'd him why he had not ordered the — King's Troops and such of the Inhabitants as could be collected to the Trenches, he said that he had ordered Colonel Etherington two hours ago to March to the Intrenchments with the King's Troops, and that he was surprised what detained him. — In the mean time Colonel Etherington rode up to the Door, and the Governor called out to him — "Did not I Order you two Hours ago to march the King's Troops to the —

Present day (2001) view from Wilkie's Battery of the Bay at Calliaqua and the Town. On the point directly across from here was the Hyde's Point Battery where the gunner's first saw the invading "French" ships on the morning of July 16, 1779. Calliaqua, in French/Spanish means "Still Waters" and was once the principle points from which sugar was shipped from St. Vincent's as most of the large estates were close to it slightly up the Windward Coast. The large island to the right is Bequia. Photo by: Co-author, Rodger Durham.

Present day view (2001) from Dorchester Hill overlooking Kingstown towards Berkshire Hill and Fort Charlotte (in 1779, the Barracks). This is where Governor Morris had proposed to make the last stand against the French and the capitulation terms were signed in 1779. Photo by: Co-author Rodger Durham.

Intrenchments"? The Colonel replied, what Intrenchments did you mean? I was surprised at the question, and could not help observing, that it must be evident what Intrenchments were meant, when they know the Enemy were landing at Sir William Young's Bay, upon which — the Colonel said, "The reason of my asking the question is, because Governor Morris was out this Morning reconnoitering, and told me that he expected a Landing of the Enemy also at Ottley's Bay; The Colonel then turn'd his Horse and said, "I'll warrant the King's Troops will be in time to do their duty and rode off." — I went away then to Town, and after being there then about an hour, I heard the Musick of the 60th Regiment coming into Town, I mounted my Horse and took a Fuzee in my hand, and went and joined them near the Custom House, The Governor and Colonel in the Front, with about fifty Men under Arms, as near as I can guess following them and eight or — nine of the Band of Musick — At this time I saw several of the — Inhabitants with their Firelocks on their Shoulders come and offer their Service to join the King's Troops, which Governor Morris forbid their doing, and ordered them to go to the Battery behind the Town, and wait his Orders; I asked him if he had sent any body to give him — information of the situation and advances of the Enemy, -- he said not, and beg'd I wou'd go, upon which I went on to Mr. Crook's Plantation, where I overtook Ensign Van Hamel of the 60th Regiment, with a Drummer on Horseback attending him; he had at this time fallen off his Horse, I asked him where he was going, he told me that Governor Morris had sent him to demand of the French Commandant what brought him there, or Words nearly to that effect, I told him it was a very ridiculous Message, he said he thought so too, but that he was obliged to obey Orders; I told him, as I had no occasion to go further, I would give him my — Horse, which I did, and then walked to a rising Ground that overlooked the Sugar Works, where the French Troops had halted; I had not been long there, before they began their March, and had a very distinct view of them; One third of them had not Cartouch Boxes, and seem'd to be very ill Arm'd; I reckoned them as near as I could, and imagined their numbers to be about Two hundred and sixty of all kinds, Troops, Volunteers, Mulattoes &c. — I saw Mr. Van Hamel meet the Officer at the Head of the French Troops who took his Horse, and Mr. Van Hamel and the Drummer went immediately to the rear; There was a small party of Men with an Officer had come very near me before I observed them; When I did, I ran as fast as I could and went into Mr. Crooks's House; by this time some of the French Troops had got into the Negroe Houses, and I — thought I should have been taken

Prisoner, but on looking out again I observed that they had not advanced so fast as I thought they would, I took up my Firelock which I had before laid by, and made the best of my way towards the Intrenchments; by the time I got there the Troops &c. had abandon'd the Hill, and were on their March back to the Battery over the Town, when I got to the top of the Hill I call'd out as loud as I could "Governor Morris! which I repeated Twice or Thrice before he attended to me, he stop'd at last until I came up, I then told him: You will be ashamed, when you see the Banditti you are giving up the Island to; for God's sake, order back the Troops to the Intrenchments, they have time — enough still to gain them before the Enemy — He said Colonel Etherington had march'd back the Troops without any Order from him which he should be answerable for, -- I then told him, "You certainly Command Colonel — Etherington, and you can order them back again: He said that it was then too late, but that he would go with the Troops to the Battery above the Town, — which he was determined to defend to the last extremity. I then observed to — him that in my opinion, by giving up the Intrenchments and that Hill, he had given up the Island, to which he made no Answer but went on to the Battery.

Q. Who Commanded the Troops on the Island of St. Vincent's?
A. The Governor gave out all Orders.

Q. Was you in the Fort at the time they were going to fire the 18 pounder?
A. I was.

Q. Who appeared to you to be Commanding Officer in the Battery?
A. I suppose the Governor was.

Q. Was the 18 pounder fired?
A. No.

Q. Who prevented it.
A. The Prisoner.

Q. For what reason?
A. He call'd to them to stop, and said, there never was such a thing heard of as firing on the Enemy when a Flag of Truce was out.

Q. Did you inform the Governor that a Flag of Truce was detain'd some time before the proposal to fire the Gun?
A. I did.

Q. Did you inform the Prisoner that the Flag was detain'd?
A. I do not recollect informing him — particularly.

Q. Was the Prisoner backward in Engaging the Enemy?
A. I thought so.

Q. What reason had you to think so?
A. Because I did not see him take any active part in encouraging the Men or Posting them.

Q. Were the Troops at Hartley's Hill time — enough to have acted against the Enemy?
A. I saw them on their March, and they had sufficient time to get there, but I was not there at the time they were.

Q. Did you hear Terms of Capitulation — proposed, and do you remember who was the proposer?
A. I heard the Prisoner talk about it.

Q. What did you hear the Prisoner say respecting a Capitulation?
A. I heard him say that it was only the Advance of the Enemy, and there was a greater Force in the rear; I had just about that moment received a letter from the Windward part of the Island — mentioning, that three Ships were in view under English Colours, and I had already said, I supposed they were Ships of the Enemy which might have induced the Prisoner to say; those landed were only an advanced — Guard of the Enemy.
Q. Did others besides yourself suppose them to be Enemy Ships?
A. Yes.

Q. Would Governor Morris have made an attempt to defend the Island had the Prisoner supported him?
A. I don't believe he wou'd.

Q. Why do you think so?
A. Because Governor Morris never took any pains to collect the Inhabitants, which he might have done, to the number of Eighty or

Ninety Men, accustomed to Arms, in the Town & Valley of Kingstown; and I observed to the Governor, there were two — Field pieces near his House which might be easily carried to the — Intrenchments, and I offered to procure Negroes for that purpose, if he wou'd give me Orders, to which the Governor gave no Answer.

Q. Whom did Governor Morris send with — proposals of Capitulation, to the Enemy?

A. The Prisoner went out, and I heard the Governor say, with a good deal of hesitation, after being much press'd, that he was privy to his going.

Q. Were the Soldiers of the 60th Regiment who were present sufficient to have check'd the Enemy had they engag'd them on the most advantageous situation the Ground afforded?

A. I cannot depend on my Judgement but I have heard the Engineer say, the Ground was strong and that a small number of Men might defend it against a much superior force.

The Court adjoured to meet to Morrow Morning
at 10 o'clock.

Tuesday 9th October 1781.

<u>Evidence</u>   **Mr. Duncan Campbell**

Q. by the Prisoner — In the course of your Evidence, you have said that it seemed backward to Engage the Enemy on the 16th June 1779; Were there any Orders given to attack the Enemy?

A. I did not hear any Orders given to attack.

Q. by the Court — Can you give any reason why that part of the 60th Regiment Quartered at the Leeward part of the Island, were not assembled to oppose the Enemy?

A. I cannot: They were far distant as not to be assembled immediately; but might have been brought up by the next Morning, and both the Governor and Prisoner were applied to for that purpose, who promised it should be done.

Q. Could the Prisoner, without the Governor's Orders, have sent for these Troops?

A. I believe so; I heard him say they were sent for when the Governor was not present.

<u>Evidence</u>   **Mr. William Richardson —**
Carpenter, having been duly sworn and examined as to the

<u>1st Charge</u>   <u>Giving in false Returns</u>
            Answ? I know nothing respecting this charge.

The Evidence being examined as to the

<u>2nd Charge</u>
            <u>Improperly employing some of the Forces &c. &c. &c.</u>

Answ? I never had an opportunity of knowing any thing about it.

<u>3rd Charge</u>
            <u>Disobeying several Orders given by said —</u>
                  <u>Governor &c. &c. &c.</u>

Answ? I know not the least about it.

<u>4th Charge</u>
            <u>Neglect of duty and improper behaviour &c. &c. &c.</u>

A. I was at St. Vincent's on the Morning the 16th of June 1779 when the French landed and I arm'd myself as did several others, and went to the Government House; when we arrived there; Governor Morris came out, and told us he had sent two or three different Messages to the Prisoner to Muster his Men but that he saw no appearance of any movement: At that Moment the Prisoner came riding up and the Governor said, for God's sake get your Men, and go up to the Intrenchments, The Prisoner immediately rode off, and we return'd again to Town, A short time afterwards Governor Morris and the Prisoner came on with about Forty Soldiers, we /the inhabitants/ then join'd the Governor and Prisoner, and proceeded along the Public Road. /The Troops being sent a bye way up the Hill,/ when we arrived upon the top of the Hill — we saw the French Troops drawn up at Mr. Brook's Works, and they soon began to advance, It was then proposed to go in to the Intrenchments: — The Governor and Prisoner stepp'd aside /as I imagined to confer/ and immediately afterwards a Person was — dispatched to order the Troops to return, and go into the Fort over the Town, upon which we /the inhabitants/ all followed them and went — into the same Fort,

The Engineer Mr. Lees then station'd Captain — Cunningham /Master of a Merchantman/ and me at a Gun, after the Gun was got ready, the French Troops having advanced to a situation where we thought a Gun might do execution, It was proposed to fire the Gun, and I think Governor Morris gave Orders to fire it. Mr. — Cunningham was going to apply the Match, when the Prisoner said to the Governor, for God's sake don't fire! You have sent a Flag of Truce which is not yet returned and it may be of bad consequence.

Q. by the court — Did the Prisoner — shew signs of fear in the face of the Enemy?
   A. I saw nothing different from his usual appearance.

Q. Did Governor Morris make any reply to the Prisoner when he desired him not to fire the Gun?
   A. I do not recollect that he did.

Q. Who dispatched the Person to order the — Troops to return?
   A. I don't recollect.

Q. by the Prisoner — How many of the Inhabitants went with the Governor and me on the Public Road up — the Hill?
   A. There might be eight or ten.

Q. by the court — Did the prisoner take any other Method to prevent the Gun to be fired, than that you have mentioned?
   A. No other.

Q. Did the Governor join in Opinion — with him about not firing the Gun?
   A. Nothing further was said or done in it.

The Evidence being examined as to the

5th Charge
            After the Capture of the said Island &c. &c. &c.

Answ? I know nothing relating to this charge.

Evidence
   Doctor John Connor late of the — Hospital at St. Vincent's being duly sworn and examined as to the

1st Charge   <u>Giving in false Returns</u>

Answ? I know not relative to this charge.

The Evidence being examined as to the

<u>2nd Charge</u>
    <u>Improperly employing, some of the Forces &c. &c &c</u>

Answ? I have seen Troops upon his Estate but know not how they were employed.

The Evidence being examined as to the

<u>3rd Charge</u>
    <u>Disobeying several Orders given by the said Governor &c. &c. &c</u>

I know nothing relating to this charge.

The Evidence being examined as to the

<u>4th Charge</u>
    <u>Neglect of duty and with improper behaviour &c. &c. &c.</u>

Answ. On the Morning of the 16th of June — 1779 I saw Doctor Glasgow, who inform'd me positively, that French Troops were disembarked at Calliqua', I beg'd he wou'd go and inform the Governor and I went to Town to inform the Inhabitants, and afterwards to the — Barracks, to acquaint the Prisoner; On my arrival there, I ask'd him if he had heard of the Enemy's landing, or if he had received any Orders in consequence from the Governor; The Prisoner told me he had Orders to — occupy the Trenches, I told him I came as a Volunteer and ask'd for a — Musket, The Prisoner told me, he had not sufficient for his own Men, and that I should be of more use in the way of my Profession — I observed that every thing should be done immediately, as I feared the French — would get possession of the Heights, — I further told him I did not think there cou'd be many of them, as there were only three Frigates, and that I was surprised no body endeavoured to find out their — strength, that it wou'd be an everlasting disgrace to have the Island taken without a shot fired. That I hoped he had sent to collect the — Troops from the Leeward of the Island, and if so, we could hold out 'till they joined. I then quitted the Prisoner and

walked in the Gallery with some of the Officers, and not perceiving
the Troops in motion, /though they might probably be so unknown to
me/ I addressed — myself again to the Prisoner and desired to
know what he intended to do, observing that if something was not
done, the Island would fall shamefully. The Prisoner said, he did not
understand Governor Morris's Orders, or what Trenches he meant,
and that he would — remain at the Barracks and defend them,
which was the only defence he was equal to, under the Command
of such a Man; I answered that if the Prisoner would take upon
himself the Defence of the Island, I wou'd undertake that the
Governor shou'd not prevent him — The Prisoner said, it was more
than he dirst do, as the Governor Commanded — and he cou'd not
lay him aside. When I found it was the Prisoner's resolution, to
remain at the Barracks, I — departed with an intention of going to
the Governor, whom I met — half way between the Government
House and Barracks, I asked him if the Island was to be given
away? and if he did not mean to make some defence? and
whether he had ordered the Troops from Leeward? he said in a
Gasconading way, he had, and added, "That he wou'd lose his last
Blood to defend the Island, and hoped all animosities would cease,
and that the Inhabitants wou'd join him in defending the Island. I
informed him that I had been with the Prisoner, who would not move
from the Barracks as he did not understand his Orders; I further
observed that if he /the Governor/ wou'd order the Guns at a Fort
called Akers to be spiked, and order the Prisoner with the Troops to
Mr. Hartley's Hill, that the inhabitants wou'd join him, & enable him
to hold out 'till the Troops from Leeward joined, and if after that, the
Enemy were superior, that he cou'd further hold out — 'till relieved
by General Grant, to whom, and to Admiral Byron I begged he
wou'd send off Expresses immediately. The Governor said he
wou'd, and complained, that he had sent repeated Orders to the
Prisoner who would not obey them, and ordered me to go and
report to him his positive Orders to March the Troops to Hartley's
Hill; I said I was not a proper Person, not being a Military Man, but
that if he would put his Orders in writing I would carry them to the
Prisoner. I recommended to him to appoint one of the Officers of
the — 60th to act as Fort Adjutant of the day, who might carry his
Orders — The Governor said he wou'd be advised by me and rode
off: I proceeded to Town where I found very few People, the greater
part as I was informed had gone for their Arms. I afterwards
returned to the Prisoner at the Barracks, and repeated the
Conversation that had passed between the Governor and myself,
and told him, the Governor complain'd much of his not possessing

Present day view (2001) overlooking the ruins of the Military Hospital that was built just below Fort Charlotte around 1806. In 1779, this area, known as Berkshire Hill (on which Fort Charlotte was later built), was the site of the Barracks where Etherington initially assembled the troops after being summoned by Governor Morris on July 16, 1779. As is evident, this hill affords a commanding view of Kingstown Bay (the city is to the left in the photo) and Bequia Island can be seen in the distance. Photo by: Co-author Rodger Durham.

View of Kingston from the road coming down from the Barracks site on Berkshire Hill (Fort Charlotte). From here, one can visualize the route that Etherington's troops and everyone else used in July 1779. Thus, the march was down the old road from the Barracks on Berkshire Hill into and throughout Town (Kingstown) on Back Street (which still exists today), up Sion Hill where Morris and Etherington argued (far right in the photo), past Mr. Hartley's House, and then turning back toward Town (middle left in the photo) and proceeding further up to Dorchester Hill above the Town. Photo by: Co-author Rodger Durham.

the Trenches according to his Orders, that the — French Troops were at that time on their March and wou'd be in possession of the Heights before him. Mr. Phipps /who acted as Aid de Camp to the Governor/ arrived at that Moment, and deliver'd Orders to the Prisoner which I know nothing of; The Prisoner told me once more, he did not see what else cou'd be done but defend the Barracks, but that he wou'd go to the Governor and see what was to be done; I then left the Prisoner and went towards the Governor's House, with an intention of speaking to the Governor. On the Road I met Mr. Reynolds /another acting Aid de Camp of the Governor's/ who had in his hand a Paper written in French, I asked him where he was going and the contents of the Paper, he told me, he was ordered to carry that Paper to the Commandant of the French Troops, and to know his business on the Island — I said the Governor was a Blockhead for sending him on such a Message to an Officer who was at the head of Troops, — with the colours of his Nation flying, and of course was come to take the Island, and that I believed the Governor meant to give it away. I told him to return, which he at first refused, but on my telling him he would be fired upon as a Spy, he seem'd alarm'd, and went back — In a short time afterwards I met the Prisoner coming — from Government House, who told me that the Troops were ordered to the Hill, and I proceeded with the Prisoner and joined the Troops. The Governor soon came up and I recommended — to him to beat to Arms, and the Inhabitants would join him — when they knew that any thing real was intended, upon which — the Drummer beat to Arms and several of the Inhabitants joined us, but the Governor did not permit them to join the Troops, but ordered them to a Fort above the Town. — As we [proceeded] through the Town, it was proposed by the Governor, and acceded to by the Prisoner to send Ensign Van Hamel with a Message to the same purpose as — that sent by Mr. Reynolds, who went in consequence. We soon — after arrived at Hartley's Hill, when we perceived the Enemy drawing up about a Quarter of a Mile distant from us, the Governor then — repeatedly ask'd what was to be done, saying, "we are a poor Council of War; and addressing himself to the People about him, said, he wished they wou'd say what was to be done, I recommended to him to address himself to the Prisoner, upon which the Prisoner said he was ready to do any thing the Governor ordered him; The Governor then proposed, and it was agreed to by all Parties, to return to the Fort above the Town, where were two 18 Pounders mounted, and a Proof Magazine adjoining, with an Artillery Store immediately below it: The Governor therefore <u>ordered the Prisoner there with the Troops.</u>

Soon after our — arrival at the Fort above the Town, the Enemy
appeared upon the — Hill that we had abandoned, few in Numbers,
and without any shew of Artillery. The Inhabitants proposed to fire
one of the 18 Pounders the other being out of Order, but were
prevented by the Governor and the Prisoner, the latter declaring it
was not customary whilst a — Flag of Truce was out, I said it was as
uncustomary to detain a — Flag of Truce and that the Officer who
was sent with it, wou'd not be permitted to return, lest he should
expose the Enemy's strength — Therefore the Inhabitants again
proposed to fire; and were prevented; The Governor said he would
send Mr. Phipps, his Aid de Camp, to demand the reason the
Enemy detained the Flag, who was accordingly sent, and returned
back from the Enemy with an Answer, that they did not consider it
as a Truce, and wou'd detain it. At the same moment we saw a
small Party of the Enemy advancing and I asked the Governor if he
meant to let them March into the Fort, and requested he would —
send an Officer and party of Men to stop them and to fire at them if
they advanced. An Officer and a party were sent, and when the
Enemy saw them they halted, at which time the Inhabitants again
proposed to fire the 18 Pounder and they were prevented by the
Governor. The Prisoner having rode at this time towards the
Enemy, Mr. Campbell and I desired the Governor wou'd inform us
where the Prisoner was going, and who sent him, The Governor,
after some hesitation, acknowledg'd that the Prisoner went with his
approbation. The Inhabitants then again proposed to the Governor
to fire the 18 Pounder, who prevented them saying, that the
Prisoner was gone to the Enemy and it might hit him. The Prisoner
soon after return'd, and after some conversation with the Governor;
The Governor declar'd that a Capitulation had been asked for, and
that he was offered the same as was granted at Dominique; The
Governor then ask'd the Inhabitants if such a Capitulation would be
agreeable to them All except two answer'd that it would not and that
they said the Island was going to be given away treacherously and
infamously, and desired the Governor to recollect, that the Island
was not taken but given away — The Governor then desired the
Prisoner to return to the Officer Commanding the French Troops,
requesting untill the next Morning to sign the — Capitulation; The
Prisoner accordingly went, and brought back Word it was agreed to;
upon which the Governor desired the Inhabitants to — return to their
respective Habitations, and said, that a Capitulation was agreed
upon, and that there was no further use for their staying where they
were; At this time many other Inhabitants who had gone home to
fetch their Arms, were on their March to join us, but on hearing that

a Capitulation was agreed upon, they dispersed and went back to their Houses — The Troops still kept possession of the Fort, and the French Frigates /having Chased a Vessel in the Morning/ fell to Leeward and cou'd not fetch back into the Bay — The Governor seeing this, seem'd sorry for what had happen'd and he and the Prisoner condemn'd each other for it; The Governor declared he did not — think himself bound to adhere to his agreement; and would — assemble all the Force he could by the next Morning, and find some means to break through it. In consequence of this several of the -- Inhabitants assembled again, Mr. Campbell and myself enquired of the Prisoner, if the Troops were coming from Leeward, and if any — thing was to be done. The Prisoner answer'd that if the Troops were ordered up, he wou'd engage they wou'd arrive in Town by nine — next Morning — On hearing that there was a Council next Morning at the Government House, I went there, and I heard the Governor at that time say to the Prisoner the following words, — "Did I not tell you Colonel two or three days ago that I had certain Information that this Island was to be attack'd," — The Prisoner said — Yes you did but you have had so many reports of the same kind that I did not believe it; and I asked the Governor why if he knew it, did he not prepare for it.

The Court adjourn'd to meet to Morrow
Morning at 10 o'clock.

Wednesday 10th October 1781

Captain Ebenezor Vavasor of the 27th Regiment one of the Members of the Court-martial being sick and unable to attend.

The Court adjourned to meet
to Morrow Morning at 10 o'clock.

Thursday 11th October 1781

Captain Ebenezor Vavasor not being able to attend, Three new members were proposed to be added to the Court-martial, to prevent future delays from sickness.

Captain Edward Chandler 27th Regiment
Captain William S. Leger 86th Regiment   New Members
Captain John Howarth 27th Regiment

Having been duly Sworn; the former Proceedings of this Court-martial were read to them in Presence of the Evidences

Evidence   **Doctor John Connor**

Q. by the court — As you have often referr'd to your Minutes, pray when did you make them?
A. To the best of my Memory a day or two after the Island of St. Vincent's was taken.

Q. Were the Barracks that the Prisoner proposed to defend, Fortified?
A. They were surrounded by a Stone Wall and there were two Field pieces.

Q. Was the Ground on which the Barracks stood a strong situation, and capable of resisting the Attack?
A. I do not think it was a strong situation.

Q. Who was charged with the Defence of the Island?
A. The Governor.

Q. What Post on the Island at that time did you imagine the most capable of Defence?
A. The Fort above the Town where the two 18 pounders were.

Q. Did the Troops occupy that Post?
A. They did.

Q. Were the Troops under Arms time enough to — occupy any of the defensible Posts about Kingston which the Governor might have ordered them to?
A. They were.

Q. Were the Troops ordered from the — Leeward part of the Island?
A. I don't know.

Q. Could the Prisoner with the — Governor's Orders, have sent for those Troops?
A. I think he cou'd not with propriety.

Q. To whom do you attribute the neglect — of calling in the Troops?

A. I think it was the Governor's business.

Q. Had the Troops from Leeward joined, wou'd your force have been sufficient to have defeated the Enemy's — Attack on the Island?

A. I think it wou'd.

Q. Had you a sufficient Force collected when the Capitulation was proposed, to have defended the Island until such time as the Troops stationed to Leeward cou'd have joined.

A. I think we had.

Q. What did your Force consist of?

A. About sixty Regulars and thirty — Militia to the best of my Recollection.

Q. Did the Prisoner shew signs of fear in the face of the Enemy?

A. I do not think he did.

Q. To the best of your knowledge, did the Prisoner do or say, any thing to induce the Governor to surrender — the Island?

A. Not to my knowledge.

Q. Did you hear the Prisoner make use of any expressions tending to discharge the Troops or Militia?

A. Nothing more than his preventing the Gun to be fired, and saying, the French Troops which appeared were only the advanced Guard.

Q. What was the Enemy's Force?

A. To the best of my knowledge, One hundred and twenty or One hundred and thirty Regulars and about — Two hundred and fifty People of different colours.

Q. Were the French Troops advancing to Mr. Hartley's Hill when our Troops retired from it.

A. I think not.

The Evidence being examined as to the

5th Charge

<u>After the Capture of said Island &c. &c. &c.</u>

Answ. I know nothing of this charge.

Evidence **Doctor Robert Glasgow** having been duly sworn and examined as to the

1st Charge <u>Giving in false Returns</u>

Answd. I know nothing relating to it.

The Evidence being examined as to the

2nd Charge
<u>Improperly employing some of the Forces &c. &c. &c.</u>

Answd. I never was upon the — Estate and know nothing of it

The Evidence being examined as to the

3rd Charge
<u>Disobeying several Orders given by the said Governor &c. &c. &c.</u>

Answd. I cannot tell any thing about the Matter.

The Evidence being examined as to the

4th Charge
<u>Neglect of duty and improper behaviour &c. &c. &c.</u>

Answd. On the Morning of the 16th June 1779 I set out to visit a Gentlemen in the Island of St. Vincent's, when I came to the Bay called Sir William Young's Bay, I saw Troops landing, which, from their dress, I judged were French, I immediately returned to give the necessary information, and met Mr. John Connor and Mr. Cunningham who return'd with me — I went immediately to the Government House, and Mr. Connor said he wou'd proceed to — acquaint the Prisoner at the Barracks, when I arrived at the Governor's I saw him and the Prisoner together and told them what I had seen at Sir William Young's Bay; they asked me whether they were French Troops I had seen; I told them positively they were; The Governor told the Prisoner to go to the Barracks immediately and March the Men down, and make the best defence possible, /or

Another view of the Bay at Calliaqua. The small island in the middle is Young's Island, previously owned by Sir William Young, the famous St. Vincent plantation owner and former Land Commissioner. The small island to the far right is Fort Duvernette, also call "The Rock", originally built by the French before British occupation of St. Vincent. Photo by: Co-author Rodger Durham.

Words to that — effect/ The Governor at the same time told the Prisoner to send off an Express to Captain Kelly of the 60th Regiment, to use every expedition to bring the Men from Chateau Bellair as the Island was attacked by the French. Upon which the Prisoner went away, I proceeded to my own House and waited there expecting the arrival of the Troops and after waiting probably an hour and a half, and seeing no appearance of the Troops, I returned to the Government House to learn the cause of the delay — I ask'd the Governor why the 60th Regiment had not — made their appearance, who told me that he had sent repeated — Messages to the Prisoner and could not account for their remaining so long at the Barracks — About this time Mr. Phipps /who acted as Aid de Camp to the Governor/ arrived, and said, that the — Prisoner had sent him to know where the Men were to be March'd to, I answered that it was impossible the Prisoner could be ignorant of it, as I had told the Governor and him the place where the French were landing. Mr. Phipps then said that there was some report that the French were also Landing to Leeward. The Prisoner at that time came himself, and I understood he came to know where the — Men were to be March'd to, and imagine he was inform'd, as I saw the Men a short time afterwards, March from their Barracks. The Troops repaired to the top of Hartley's Hill, where they remained a very short time, and before I got there, they were march'd away, and I — understood went to occupy a little Fort behind the Town of Kingston. Before the Troops went up Hartley's Hill I understood that Ensign Van Hamel was sent to the Enemy with a Flag of Truce. I then went to the Fort which the Troops were gone to and joined by several Inhabitants who with Lieutenant Lees were busy pointing a Gun towards the Road which it was thought the French must pass — after waiting near three–Quarters of an Hour, the French made their appearance upon Hartley's Hill, and began to March down the Road towards Kingston, at which — time I was much surprised, and so were others, to see the Prisoner — ride off towards the French, and I heard the Governor say, "where can he be going to? The Prisoner went up, and spoke to the Commandant of the French Troops, and after staying several Minutes he returned, and soon afterwards I saw the French Commander coming towards the Fort. When the Prisoner return'd I heard him speak of a Capitulation, saying that very good Terms wou'd be granted, and that it wou'd be the best thing that could ever happen to the Island — At this time a considerable Number of the Charibs appear'd upon the top of Hartley's Hill, which alarm'd those Inhabitants who had Estates thereabouts, some of whom were at that time in the Fort and they wished for a Capitulation saying, the Charibs would burn and destroy every thing; other inhabitants opposed it, saying it — would be a shame the Island shou'd be given up to the Troops who had come against it, — I forgot to mention, that when the Prisoner was with the Enemy, several of the Inhabitants wanted to fire the Gun, but were prevented /I believe/ by Governor Morris, who, I think said, that if the Enemy advanced any further it should be fired. — On the same Night I heard Governor Morris say, that he had ask'd until ten o'clock next day to sign the Capitulation, by which time he expected Captain Kelly up from Leeward with the Troops, and that he wou'd call a Council to — deliberate on the Terms proposed by the French Governor, or Words to — that effect, and I believe the Capitulation was signed the next day, and that Captain Kelly did not arrive from Leeward with the Troops the 17th.

Q. by the Court — Was any body present, when the Governor told the Prisoner to March to the Intrenchments and make the best defence he cou'd, and when he directed him to send an Express to Captain Kelly to March with the Troops from Leeward?
A. I don't recollect any Persons being present except myself.

Q. You have mentioned that the Troops march'd up Hartley's Hill and down again, — by whose Orders did they march down?
A. I don't know.

Q. When the Prisoner rode towards the Enemy, was it by his own accord, or by Order of the Governor?
A. I imagine it was not by Order of the Governor, as he expressed a surprise on seeing him go.

Q. Did you hear any Conversation between the Governor and the Prisoner before the Prisoner went out to the — Enemy?
A. They might have been in conversation together, but I did not hear it.

Q. Did the Governor call him back?
A. I don't know.

Q. Cou'd he have call him back?
A. When I saw him, he cou'd not.

Q. Who was present at the Battery, when the Governor expressed his surprise at the Prisoner riding towards the Enemy?

A. Mr. Duncan Campbell, Mr. John Connor, Mr. Bolton, and Mr. Richardson.

Q. Did the Enemy advance after the Prisoner went to them?
A. I believe not.

Q. Did you see the Prisoner after his return from the Enemy?
A. Yes.

Q. Had he any Conversation with the — Governor after his return?
A. I saw them together, but did not hear their Conversation.

Q. Was the Capitulation determined upon on the 16th of June?
A. Not that I heard of.

Q. Did the French Commandant sup with the Governor the night of the 16th?
A. I know not whether he supp'd, but I saw — him at the Governor's.

Q. Did you sup there?
A. I have forgot.

Q. Was the Prisoner there?
A. I do not recollect.

Q. Did you ever hear the Governor at any time acknowledge, that he was privy to the Prisoner's going to the French — Commandant?
A. I did not.

The Court adjourned to meet
to Morrow Morning at 10 o'clock.

Friday 12th October 1781

Evidence   **Doctor Robert Glasgow**

Q. by the Court — Did you see the French Commandant in the Fort on the Evening of the 16th?
A. I saw him very near it.

Q. Did you hear the Governor, or Prisoner, say any thing on the Evening of the 16th respecting a Capitulation?

A. I heard the Governor say they were preparing a Capitulation, but I did not hear the Prisoner say any thing about it.

Q. Who were the Company then present?
A. I don't know.

Q. Was the Prisoner there?
A. I think not.

Q. Did the French Commandant remain the whole Night with the Governor?
A. I left the Governor's House early & do not know.

Q. What numbers did the Enemy consist of.
A. I heard there were Two hundred and fifty, beside the Charibbs.

Q. Where were the King's Troops on the night of the 16th?
A. I think they remained at the Fort?

Q. Did the Prisoner give any reason for his saying that a Capitulation was the best thing that cou'd happen to the Island?
A. He said, that if the Island was — retaken, the Charibbs wou'd be driven off the Island, as they had taken an active part.

Q. Who prevented the Gun from being — fired when the Prisoner was gone out to meet the Enemy?
A. The Governor.

Q. What reasons did he give for preventing it?
A. I did not hear any.

Q. Was the Prisoner present when the Governor said he wanted to gain time 'till Captain Kelly arrived — with the Troops?
A. I believe not.

Q. Did the Prisoner send off to Captain Kelly agreeable to the Governor's Orders?
A. I don't know.

Q. At what time did the Governor give the Prisoner Orders to send for Captain Kelly?

A. Between ten and eleven in the Morning.

Q. Did the Governor mention any thing to the Prisoner about the Enemy's Landing to Leeward?

A. Not in my presence.

Q. Did you ever hear the Governor express a disapprobation of the Prisoner's Conduct, when the Prisoner was present?

A. No.

Q. At the time the Prisoner was out with the Enemy had you any Conversation with the Governor?

A. No.

Q. Did you know if the Prisoner made a proposal, of any Mode of defence to the Governor, before the Capitulation was agreed upon?

A. I don't know.

Q. Who sign'd the Capitulation?

A. Governor Morris.

Q. Who had the defence of the Island?

A. Governor Morris.

Q. Would the Prisoner have defended the Island had the Governor supported him?

A. From the delay of the Troops and his going to the Enemy I did not think he shew'd any Zeal to defend the Island.

Q. Do you know that the Prisoner made any unnessary delay with the Troops?

A. It was between ten and eleven o'clock when he received Orders from the Governor, and Imagine it was about two o'clock when they March'd from the Barracks.

Q. At what time was the Gun first pointed, and proposed to be fired?

A. About four o'clock.

Q. Had the Prisoner proposed to the Governor to take the Command for the defence of the Island on the 16th, have you — reason to think that the Governor wou'd have agreed to it?
A. I believe he wou'd.

Q. What are your reasons for so thinking?
A. From the general tenor of his Conversation to me on that subject.

Q. Did he tell you he wou'd have given the — Command up to the Prisoner?
A. He did not.

Q. Do you know that he asked the Prisoner's advice about the defence of the Island?
A. I do not.

Q. At what time did the Prisoner go out the first time, to meet the Enemy?
A. I believe about four o'clock.

The Evidence being examin'd relative to the

<u>5th Charge</u>
<u>After the Capture of said Island &c. &c. &c.</u>

Ansd. I know nothing respecting this — charge.

<u>Evidence</u>
John Bolton Shopkeeper at St. Vincent's having been duly sworn and examined as to the

<u>1st Charge</u>   <u>Giving in false Returns</u>

Ansd. I know nothing about it.

The Evidence being examin'd as to the

<u>2nd Charge</u>
<u>Improperly employing some of the Forces &c. &c. *c</u>

Ansd. I know nothing relative to it.

The Evidence being examin'd as to the

3rd Charge
Disobeying several Orders by the said Governor &c. &c. &c.

Ansd. I know nothing about it

The Evidence being examined as to the

4th Charge
Neglect of duty and improper behaviour &c. &c. &c.

A. On the Morning of the 16th of June — 1779, about Eleven o'clock, I was in the Battery behind the Town of — Kingston where the Prisoner was; after being there some little time the French Troops made their appearance upon Hartley's Hill and were marching towards the Town; at this time the Prisoner went out by the desire of the Governor, and returned again very soon seemingly much alarm'd, and urged a Capitulation; at the same time observing that — the French Troops which then appeared were only an Advanced Party.

Q. by the Court — Did you hear the Governor order the Prisoner to go to the Enemy?
A. Yes.

Q. Do you know for what purpose he went?
A. I conceived, it was to propose a Capitulation.

Q. In what manner did the Prisoner urge a Capitulation?
A. By supposing the French Troops were so much superior.

Q. In what manner did the Prisoner appear to be alarmed?
A. By his urging a Capitulation, and his observing that it was only an advanced party of the French.

Q. What was the Opinion of others in the Fort respecting the necessity for a Capitulation?
A. I only observed two or three of the Inhabitants who seem'd to wish for a Capitulation.

Q. Did the Governor express his Sentiments upon the subject?
A. I don't recollect.

Q. Did you imagine the Party of the French, which the Prisoner said was but an advanced Party, were coming to attack you?
A. Yes.

Q. Were the Troops at the Battery time enough to have fired upon the Enemy, had they been ordered?
A. They had been there some time before the Enemy appeared on Hartley's Hill.

Q. Were not others of the same Opinion with the Prisoner, that it was only an advanced Party of the Enemy?
A. I cannot say.

Q. Do you recollect the Hour that the Prisoner went out to the Enemy?
A. To the best of my remembrance it was half past Eleven o'clock.

Q. What was the strength of the Enemy?
A. About three hundred, Mulattoes &c. &c.

Q. What was our strength at the Fort?
A. Forty three Regulars and about Thirty Inhabitants.

Q. Do you know when the Capitulation — was agreed upon?
A. About three or four o'clock in the — Afternoon the French Commandant came to the Court House in the — Town of Kingston where was a Lawyer named Burke, who I believe — was to draw out the Terms of Capitulation, and I saw the Governor and the Prisoner go there about an hour afterwards.

Q. Do you know any thing that pass'd — afterwards?
A. No, I went home.

Q. by the Prisoner — Did I go into the Court House with the Governor?
A. I don't recollect that you went in — with him, but I saw you there together some time afterwards.

The Evidence being examined as to the

5th Charge

<u>After the Capture of said Island &. &c. &c.</u>

Answd. I know nothing relative to this Charge.

<u>Evidence</u>
Doctor Patrick Connor having been duly sworn and examined as to the

1st Charge   <u>Giving in false Returns</u>

Ansd. I know nothing about this Charge.

The Evidence being examined as to the

2nd Charge
<u>Improperly employing some of the Forces &c. &c. &c.</u>

Answd. There was a detachment of the 60th Regiment posted at a place called the Ravine, on the Prisoner's Land, on Morne Garow, and they had Hutts on a flat above, and I have seen these Troops cutting down Wood but I cannot tell whether it was for the Prisoner's own private benefit or not.

Q. By whose Orders were these Troops posted on the Prisoner's Land.
A. I do not know, but the Governor knew there were Troops there, for I have rode with him over the Ground often.

Q. How many Soldiers were there?
A. Twenty five or thirty.

Q. Do you know whether any Public Works were carrying on there?
A. I have heard that a Barrack was proposed to to be built.

Q. Do you think that the Ground which the — Soldiers were clearing of the Wood, was a situation for a Barrack?
A. A very good one.

Q. Was the Wood that was cut down proper for building Barracks?
A. Some of it was.

Q. Did you ever see any of the 60th Regiment employ'd in burning and cleaning the Prisoner's Grounds?

A. I have seen fires upon his Grounds, but — never went near them.

Q. What number of Men were there at the time the Enemy Landed?

A. I believe between thirty and forty.

Q. Who Commanded those Men?

A. Captain Kelly of the 60th.

Q. Were those Men properly arm'd and appointed for Service?

A. By what I saw of their Arms, I think they were not.

Q. How often have you seen Soldiers cutting, Wood?

A. Frequently, in the course of some Weeks.

The Evidence being examined as to the

3rd Charge

Disobeying several Orders &c. &c. &c.

Answerd. I know nothing concerning it.

The Evidence being examined as to the

4th Charge

Neglect of duty and improper behaviour &c. &c. &c.

Answd. I was not present, being at the Post of Chatteaubellair.

Q. At what time did you hear of the — Enemy's landing?

A. About nine or ten o'clock the Morning of the 16th.

Q. Did Captain Kelly receive any Orders to March that day?

A. He received no Orders that I know of.

Q. What space of time would it require — for him, to have joined the Prisoner with the Detachment?

A. By great exertions he might have — joined in the course of a day by land.

Q. Was it possible for him to have joined by Water?
A. There cou'd have been conveyances by Water, provided.

Q. How long wou'd an Express be in going from Kingston to Chatteau Bellair?
A. By Land, an Express on Horseback, might go in five Hours; and on foot, in eight or nine hours.

Q. When did you first hear that the — Capitulation was agreed upon?
A. On the Evening of the 16th June 1779.

Q. Did the Troops posted at the Ravine on the Prisoner's Estate, join Captain Kelly on hearing of the Enemy's landing?
A. Yes with great dispatch.

The Evidence being examined as to the

5th Charge
After the Capture of said Island &c. &c. &c.

Ansd. I know nothing about this Charge.

Evidence   **Mr. George Fraser** Deputy Commissary General being duly sworn and examined as to the

1st Charge   Giving in false Returns

Answd. I know nothing about it.

The Evidence being examined as to the

2nd Charge
Improperly employing some of the Forces &c. &c. &c.

Ansd. I never saw any thing of it.

The Evidence being examined as to the

3rd Charge
Disobeying several Order's &c. &c. &c.

I never heard that he did.

The Evidence being examin'd as to the

4th Charge
   Neglect of duty and improper behaviour &c. &c.

Answd. On the Morning of the 16th June 1779 after I had seen the Enemy Landing, I went to the Governor's, and afterwards to the Prisoner, whom I met on the Road; and I proceeded on to the Barracks, where I apply'd for Arms, but was inform'd there were no spare Arms, I went afterwards with the Troops to the Town; Governor Morris stop'd the Troops in the Town, and sent off Ensign Van Hamel with a Flag to the Enemy; I begg'd Mr. Campbell to supply me with Arms & Ammunition which he did: By the time I was equip'd, I found the Troops were gone up Hartley's Hill, and I mounted my Horse and follow'd the Inhabitants who were going to that Hill by the main Road, When I got near the top I met two or three, who told me they were ordered to return to the Battery above the Town, which I did not believe, 'till I met Governor Morris who told me that the Troops were return'd, and that we must all go to the Battery above the Town. Soon afterwards the French were seen — Marching upon the top of Hartley's Hill, some of whom were descending the Hill and I saw the Prisoner ride out and meet them — I don't recollect any thing particular that happened until four o'clock in the afternoon when a Cessation of Arms took place, and it was agreed upon that the Capitulation shou'd be sign'd at ten o'clock the next Morning.

   Q. At what time in the Morning did you first see the British Troops under Arms?
   A. About Eleven o'clock.

   Q. Who ordered the Troops to March down — from Hartley's Hill?
   A. I don't know.

   Q. Do you attribute the loss of the Island — of St. Vincent's to the Prisoner?
   A. I cannot attribute the loss of the Island to the Prisoner, not knowing how far he was bound to obey the Governor.

   Q. Cou'd he have acted with the Troops — independent of the Governor?

A. I don't know.

Q. Did the Governor on the 16th of June give any Orders for the Troops to act?
A. I don't know.

Q. Did the Prisoner shew a proper Zeal to defend the Island, or otherwise?
A. I cannot pretend to determine upon it.

Q. Did you ever hear the Governor censure the Prisoner's Conduct on that day?
A. I never did.

Q. Was the Prisoner sent by the Governor to the Enemy?
A. Upon the Governor's being ask'd whether the Prisoner was gone to the Enemy by his Orders, he reply'd, after some hesitation, that he went by his Orders.

Q. What did the Prisoner say at his return had happened between him and the French Commandant?
A. I don't recollect.

The Evidence being examined as to the

5th Charge   After the Capture of the said Island &c. &c. &c.

Answd. I know nothing concerning it.

The Court adjourned to meet to Morrow
Morning at 10 o'clock.

Saturday 13th October 1781

Evidence   **Mr. Henry Wilkie** having been duly sworn
and examined as to the

1st Charge   Giving in false Returns

Ansd. I know nothing about it.

The Evidence being examined as to the

2nd Charge
Improperly employing some of the Forces &c. &c. &c.

Ansd. About the beginning of April 1779, Mr. Byers, a Surveyor, at St. Vincent's was employed with me, to settle the Boundaries between two Gentlemen's Estates at Chatteaubellair, whilst we were employ'd in this business, we rode one day to the Prisoner's Land, where we saw — some Hutts, Mr. Byers met there a Corporal who knew him, and of whom Mr. Byers enquired, how many People were there? The Corporal said there were sixty odd Rank and File, — I saw in different places saw'd Boards and Scantlings, but I saw nobody at Work as it was Sunday: Mr. Byers observed to the Corporal that they were a fine set of Fellows, and the Corporal said they were the finest Fellows in the Regiment; soon after which we went away.

Q. How many Men did you see on the Prisoner's Land?
A. I saw from Twenty to Twenty five.

Q. Were the Scantlings and Boards you saw there, proper for building Barracks?
A. Yes.

Q. Do you know if a Barracks was intended to be built on that Land?
A. I never heard there was.

Q. Do you know for what use these Boards and — Scantlings were intended?
A. No.

Q. Was the Prisoner's Land prepared for Sugar Cane Plants?
A. No, it was not the Trees were only just cut down.

The Evidence being examined as to the

3rd Charge
Disobeying several Orders &c. &c. &c.

Answd. I know nothing relating to it.

The Evidence being examined as to the

4th Charge
> Neglect of duty and improper behaviour &c. &c. &c.

> Ansd. I know not the least about it.

> The Evidence being examined as to the

5th Charge
> After the Capture of said Island &c. &c. &c.

> Ans. I know nothing of it.

Evidence   **Captn. Kelly** of His Majesty's 60th Regiment being duly sworn and examined as to the

1st Charge   Giving in false Returns

> Answd. I never knew any such thing.

Q. /by the Prisoner/ Did you send Monthly Returns to Governor Morris and duplicates of them to me?

A. I did.

> The Evidence being examin'd as to the

2nd Charge
> Improperly employing some of the Forces &c. &c. &c.

Answd. In the Month of October 1778 I was detach'd to Chatteaubellair and a Serjeant and twelve Men were — ordered from my Post by Governor Morris to the Prisoner's Land, and I also received orders to assist those Men with any numbers more that might be wanted to clear the Ground and build Hutts for the Men, as a Battery was intended to be made there; and I was also ordered to furnish those People with Provisions from Chatteaubellair.

Q. by the Court — Were the Orders you received for sending the Men to the Prisoner's Land, written or Verbal?
A. They were written Orders signed by the Fort Adjutant.

Q. How long were the Men continued there employed?
A. Until the Capture of the Island.

Q. Did you ever receive Orders from the Governor to withdraw the Men from the Prisoner's Estate?
A. Never.

Q. Who Commanded the Troops, and gave Orders — with respect to their distribution on the Island?
A. Governor Morris.

Q. By whose Orders were you detached to Chatteaubellair?
A. By Governor Morris's.

The Evidence being examined as to the

3rd Charge

Disobeying several Orders &c. &c. &c.

Ansd. I know nothing of it.

The Evidence being examined as to the

4th Charge
Neglect of duty and improper behaviour &c. &c.

A. I know of no neglect of duty; and as to improper behaviour in the face of the Enemy, I cannot speak to it, as I was at — Chatteaubellair when the Enemy Landed.

Q. by the Court — How many Men had you under your Command at Chatteaubellair?
A. Forty nine when the Enemy landed, and twenty five detached to the Prisoner's Land.

Q. What distance is the Prisoner's Land from — Chatteaubellair?
A. About two Miles.

Q. When did you first hear of the Enemy's Landing?
A. It was reported to me by Doctor Patrick Connor, about Twelve o'clock A: M: on the 16th June 1779.

Q. Did you receive any Orders to March with your Detachment to Kingston?

A. I received a Letter from the Prisoner to have my detachment in readiness to March at a <u>Moments warning.</u>

Q. At what time did you receive that Letter?
A. About ten or eleven at Night.

Q. In how short a time cou'd you have marched from your Post to Kingston?
A. It would have been a great March to have effected it between Sun rising, and setting, the Roads were so bad.

Q. Did you receive any other Letter?
A. I received a Letter two or three days afterwards from the Prisoner, acquainting me that the Capitulation was sign'd and ordering me to March the Detachment to Kingston.

Q. Was that the first information you had of the Capitulation?
A. It was the first positive information; there was a report of it I did not believe.

Q. Did you in consequence of the report of the French landing, call in the Out Post?
A. In consequence of Doctor Connor's — Report to me, I ordered the Men who were at the Prisoner's Land to join me immediately.

Q. Were the Troops under your Command at Chatteaubellair properly arm'd and fit for Service?
A. Yes, except for four or five who had no Arms.

Q. How many Troops were on the Island?
A. Between two and three hundred.

Q. Had you been ordered to join at Kingston by Water, cou'd you have procured Boats?
A. No.

Q. Do you know whether the Prisoner ever gave any Orders respecting the distribution of the Troops, without the Governor's knowledge?
A. No.

Evidence　　　　　　　**Ensign Van Hamel** of His Majesty's 60th
Regiment being duly sworn and examined as to the

1st Charge　　　　　　Giving in false Returns

Answd. I know nothing about it.

Q. by the Prisoner — Did you send Monthly returns to Governor
Morris, and duplicates of them to me?
Ansd. I did.

The Evidence being examined as to the

2nd Charge　　　Improperly employing some of the Forces &c. &c.

A. I know there was a Post established on the Prisoner's Land,
but I never saw any Man work there.

Q. Was you ever there?
A. Yes.

Q. By whose Order was the Post established?
A. By Governor Morris's Orders.

Q. Did any of the Soldiers complain to the Governor of Council
that they were oblig'd to work upon the Prisoner's Land?
A. I never heard that they did.

The Evidence being examined as to the

3rd Charge　　　　　　Disobeying several Orders &c. &c. &c.

An[s]d. I never heard of any disobedience of Orders.

The Evidence being examined as to the

4th Charge　　　Neglect of duty and improper behaviour &c. &c. &c.

An[s]d. I never heard the Words mention'd 'till I came to this Hill.
I beg the Court will allow me to relate from Notes and Remarks I
made at Martinique a very little time after the Capture of St.
Vincent's of every thing I saw, and that, came to my knowledge on
that day viz.

On the 16th of June 1779 being in the Town of Kingston about Nine o'clock in the Morning I heard of an Enemy Landing near the Village Calliqua, on which I made the best of my way to the Barracks, where I found the Soldiers employ'd in filling their — Pouches with Ammunition and fixing their Flints &c. Whilst they were busy about this, Mr. Phipps, an Aid de Camp to Governor Morris, came up to Colonel Etherington with Orders — I heard then that the Troops were not to March 'till said Mr. Phipps had returned from Rothia, where he was sent by Order of the Governor, it being reported the Enemy had made another Landing there; In about three quarters of an hour Mr. Phipps returned saying there was no Enemy at Rothia — The Troops fell in and march'd down to Kingston. On our March we were overtaken by Governor Morris near the Church, he assumed the Command and made a Pompous Speech to the Troops; and a little — after this he called to me and ordered me to go as a Flag of Truce to the Enemy, and to ask of them whether they came with hostile intentions, who Commanded their Troops, and desire them not to advance any further 'till they had heard again from the Governor; As I was hesitating some time on receiving such directions, the Governor repeated these again and told me, Sir, it is my positive Orders you go off immediately and take a Drummer with you; I made my bow; a Horse was procured for me, a Drummer was likewise mounted, and we proceeded towards — Calliqua. — Coming near Mr. Crooks's House the Girth of my Saddle broke and I got off having told Mr. Duncan Campbell the errand I — was sent upon, he very politely offered me his Horse, on which I proceeded towards the French — I fell in a little time after this with a reconnoitring party consisting of an Officer /whose Name I learn'd afterwards was — Canonge/ and about Twenty Men, who conducted me to the Troops which were laying on their Arms near the Negroe Houses of said Mr. Crooks's Estate two Miles from Town; I delivered part of my Message to their — Commanding Officer to which he answer'd with a smile, that he came to subdue the Island, under the Obedience of His most Christian Majesty and that his Name was Frolong Durumain &c. Fully satisfied as to the truth of his reply /after casting an Eye over the Troops/ I mounted my Horse again, but as I was going back I was stop'd by Monsieur Canonge who desired me to return to Mons. Frolong Durumain and advised him not to let me go back to Kingston, which he approved of — I was then ordered to alight, as was likewise the Drummer to which I objected in vain by saying it was against the Custom of War to detain a Flag of Truce, and I was given in charge of the Grenadiers and marched — with them in the from of the Troops —

They moved on very slowly, with reconnoitring partys advanced, and halted near the summet of Mr. Hartley's Hill, — They were joined in a short time by about Five hundred Charibbs arm'd with Fuzee and Cutlass, The French moved down towards the Town and I was left with the Drummer on the Hill near Mr. Hartley's House in charge of a Serjeant and I think fifteen or sixteen Men, who form'd a Circle around me, and the Serjeant received positive Orders not to let me come so near the brow of the Hill as to discover any thing that was going forward in Kingston I was soon afterwards removed and kept confined in Mr. — Hartley's House, 'till next Morning when I was released by the first Article of the Capitulation — I remember further that the next Morning on my coming to Kingston I went into the Court House where I saw the Governor with the Capitulation in his hand addressing himself to some of his Council a Mr. Hewit the Receiver General, and several other Town's People, in these Words, — viz. "Gentlemen, I have done all in my Power to get you the Capitulation of Dominica which I am happy I have obtained." They all congratulated him upon the occasion, and say'd they were very much — obliged to him.

Q. At what time did the Troops get under Arms?
A. A little after ten, but wou'd have march'd much sooner, if they had not been order'd to wait 'till Mr. Phipps return'd from reconnoitring the Bay of Rothia.

Q. How was the Post above the Town fortified?
A. I never was at it.

Q. Did any of the Officers of the 60th censure the Prisoner's Conduct that day?
A. No I never heard it, and had the Prisoner disobeyed any Orders on that day, or behav'd ill, the Governor having the Command it wou'd most undoubtedly have been known to me and every Person at St. Vincent's.

Q. How were the Men provided with — Ammunition before they left the Barrack's on the 16th June 1779?
A. They had plenty, I saw them provided myself.

The Evidence being examined as to the

5th Charge   After the Capture of said Island &c. &c. &c.

Ansd. I know nothing about it.

Evidence   **Serjeant Major Ayres** of His Majesty's
60th Regiment having been duly sworn and examined as to the

1st Charge   Giving in false Returns
Answd. I never heard of any.

Q. From what were the Monthly Distributions made for Governor
Morris?
A. From the monthly returns of the Officers commanding at the
different Posts.

The Evidence being examined as to the

2nd Charge
Improperly employing some of the Forces &c. &c. &c.

Answd. I know there were Men employed there,
and I knew there was a Post established there.

The Evidence being examined as to the

3rd Charge   Disobeying several Orders &c. &c. &c.

I never heard he did.

The Evidence being examined as to the

4th Charge
Neglect of duty and improper behaviour &c. &c. &c.

Ansd. On the 16th June 1779 between nine and ten o'clock I
was on the Parade and there was a rumour amongst the Men that
the Enemy had landed at Calliqua, upon which I ordered — them to
get ready the Prisoner not being then in the Barracks, but soon after
he came in great haste and confirmed the report of their Landing,
and ordered the Men to get ready and to be compleated as soon as
possible with what they wanted, Ammunition, &c.

About a quarter of an hour afterwards Mr. Phipps, an Aid de
Camp, came up to the Prisoner and spoke to him, and afterwards
he rode away. We then heard the Enemy had made also a Landing
to Leeward — The Prisoner got his Horse and rode to the

Government — House, and about 18 minutes afterwards, he
returned and ordered the Men to fall in, but a very heavy shower of
rain obliged them to shelter — themselves — Mr. Phipps came up
soon after and said the Men must March immediately, The Prisoner
then order'd the Men to March which we did very quickly whilst we
were on the March the Governor came up and said something
encouraging to the Men; Immediately after, I — heard him call for
Ensign Van Hamel repeatedly, and also heard him ask for a Horse
for the Ensign, and another for a Drummer — When the — Ensign
and Drummer were mounted they rode off — At that time the
Governor came to the front of the Troops and marched with them
through the Town of Kingston; the Troops were ordered to ascend
Hartley's Hill, by a bye road and the Governor and others went up
the high Road, when we had got up the Hill, There was a general
cry out for the Troops to go back — the Troops went back and
proceeded to a Hill above the Town where there was a Battery;
Soon after our arrival there, the Governor, the Prisoner and many
other Gentlemen join'd us a little a little afterwards, the Enemy
appeared on Hartley's Hill, and an Officer and a party were ordered
to go /by Governor Morris/ towards the Enemy as an advanced
Guard but the — Officer was very soon call'd back and received
some Orders from the Governor and afterwards went to the Enemy
who were then coming down the Hill, and a Corporal who spoke the
French Language was sent after him, both of whom I saw go to an
Officer of the Enemy who was advanced and I saw our Officer rejoin
his own Party and the Corporal who was the Interpretor came up to
the Governor I Very soon after saw the Governor and Prisoner talk
together upon the Battery where we were, after which the Prisoner
took his Horse and went to the Enemy with whom he stay'd some
little time and return'd to the Governor; soon after I heard the
Governor call the Gentlemen of the Island into a small House in the
Battery and I approach'd the Window, and heard him ask their
Opinion what he should do, they in general spoke against defending
the Island and wanted a Capitulation, which I thought from their
Conversation was agreed upon. — As soon as the Governor came
out of the House he call'd to the Prisoner and sent him off again to
the Enemy — some Inhabitants who had not been in the House
asked him what he — had resolved upon and what he wou'd do —
The Governor said he had ordered the Prisoner to obtain for them
the Capitulation of Dominique and said he was to ask two or three
more Articles which if the Enemy wou'd not grant he was to take the
Dominique — Capitulation, The Prisoner went to the Enemy and
talk'd a while with them and afterwards return'd and made his report

View from the porch of the remains of Mr. Hartley's Great House on Sion Hill (or Hartley's Hill). It looks directly southward at where Wilkie's Battery was, located in about in the middle of the picture. Photo by: Co-author Rodger Durham.

Ruins of Mr. Hartley's House on Sion Hill (or Hartley's Hill) as they appear today (2001). It was eventually taken over much later by a church, which subsequently burned down. This is what remains of the original house, as unfortunately, lack of funding has deterred archaeology and restoration interests at St. Vincent's. Photo by: Co-author Rodger Durham.

to the — Governor. The Governor mention'd aloud what he had done and added that he had obtained the Capitulation of Dominique and afterwards mounted his Horse and went to Town followed, by the Inhabitants — The Troops remained in the Battery 'till the Colours were struck — the next day.

Q. What time did the Troops march out of their Barracks?
A. I believe it was between ten and eleven o'clock.

Q. How many Men had you.
A. About forty seven.

Q. Were they properly appointed as Soldiers?
A. They were.

Q. How many Inhabitants join'd the Troops in the Battery above the Town?
A. About thirty.

Q. How many of them were arm'd?
A. I believe about ten or twelve.

Q. How is the Hill above the Town Fortified?
A. It is a Battery 'en Barbette with — two or three Guns, and was calculated to defend the Bay.

Q. Do you know whether any Charibbs — joined the Enemy?
A. I was informed there were about — Four hundred and I saw some small parties upon the Neighboring Hills.

Q. Where was the remainder of the three Companies of the 60th Regiment?
A. At the different Post upon the Island.

Q. By whose Order?
A. By the Governor's.

Q. What was the Enemy's Force?
A. I saw about three or four hundred.

Q. Amongst your Men and Officers did any — disapprove of the Prisoner's Conduct?
A. No.

Q. by the Prisoner — How were the Men provided with Ammunition before they left the Barracks?
A. They were plentifully provided.

Q. Was you present when the Governor ordered me the first and second time to the Enemy?
A. I was.

Q. What did the Governor say when I returned to him the second time from the Enemy?
A. The Governor said he was happy to have got the Capitulation of Dominica, and he told the Inhabitants that they — might return to their Homes.

Q. by the Court — Did you as Serjeant — Major see all the returns that were made of the Troops on the Island?
A. I saw a good many of them but not all having been sometimes detach'd from head Quarters — but I saw all Returns for the last fourteen Months, except when I happened to be sick.

The Evidence being examined as to the

5th Charge   After the Capture of said Island &c. &c. &c.

A. I know nothing relating to it.

Evidence   **Serjt. John Mc Mullan** of His — Majesty's 60th Regiment being duly sworn and examined as to the

1st Charge   Giving in false Returns

Answd. I know nothing about it.

The Evidence being examin'd as to the

2nd Charge   Improperly employing some of the Forces &c. &c. &c.
Ansd. I know nothing relating to it.

The Evidence being examined as to the

3rd Charge   Disobeying several Orders &c. &c. &c.

I never heard he did until I came here.

The Evidence being examined as to the

4th Charge   Neglect of duty and improper behaviour &c. &c. &c.

Ansd. I know of no neglect of duty, and I never saw any improper behaviour in the Prisoner. — On the day of the 16th of June 1779 the Governor was present with the Troops, and he never gave the Order to Fight, or make any resistance, therefore the Prisoner could not behave ill.

Q. At what time were the Troops under Arms?
A. Between ten and eleven o'clock.

Q. Were they upon the Battery time enough to have fired upon the Enemy had the Governor ordered them?
A. Yes.

Q. Were the Men properly arm'd for defence?
A. Yes.

Q. Did you perceive any dissatisfaction — amongst the Officers or Soldiers of the 60th Regiment at the Prisoner's Conduct on the day of the 16th June 1779?
A. I did not.

Q. by the Prisoner — How were the Men provided with Ammunition before they left the Barracks on the 16th June 1779?
A. I took the Cartridges out of the Store and — delivered plenty to each Man.

Q. Was you present when the Governor order'd me the first and second time to the Enemy?
A. Yes.

Q. What did the Governor say when I returned to him the second time from the Enemy?
A. He told the Inhabitants that he was happy to have obtained the Capitulation of Dominica for them and that they might go home.

The Evidence being examined as to the

5th Charge   After the Capture of said Island &c. &c. &c.

Ansd. I never heard he did.

Evidence   **Doctor George Young** being duly sworn
the following Question was put first to him by the Prisoner.

Q. When the Governor, you and some others of — the Council
were preparing the Capitulation was I there?
A. No.

Q. by the President to the D: J: Advocate — Were the Officers
of the 60th Regiment inform'd that a General Court-martial was to
be held on the Prisoner, and that all Evidences were to attend?
A. Yes, the Commander in Chief announced — this Trial in
public Orders, dated at Head Quarters the 30th September 1781.

The Prosecution being closed the — Prisoner requested the
Court would suffer him to delay entering upon his Defence until
Tuesday next.

The Prisoner's request was granted and the Court adjourned to
meet again on Tuesday Morning at Ten O'Clock.

Tuesday 16th October 1781

The Court met according to adjournment

The Prisoner not being yet sufficiently prepared to begin his
Defence, The Court adjourn'd to meet again on Thursday.

Thursday 18th October 1781.

The Court met according to adjourment and the Prisoner was put
upon his Defence.

Prisoner's Defence

Mr. President and Gentlemen of the Court —

Before I enter into a vindication of my Conduct I beg the Indulgence of the Court to speak a few Words — concerning the unfavourable circumstances under which I appear — before you.

After upwards of Thirty seven Years — constant Service, I am charg'd by a Civil Governor with a variety of Crimes which if true, wou'd be greatly aggravated by the means I — have had from long experience of knowing my duty.

It is some consolation to me that I may lament my Misfortune in the presence of Gentlemen whose Honorable feelings will not deny the tribute of Commisseration to the unfortunate.

With as much brevity as possible Mr. President I shall make my observations on each Charge in Order; — though, they appear so evidently malicious, and so totally unsupported, that I should entirely disregard them were it not for Governor Morris's industry in propagating Stories to my prejudice, and endeavouring to ruin my Character; therefore in order to have cleared to the World, I shall proceed without further delay, to observe on the

1st Charge   Giving in false Returns

To this Charge tho nothing has been proved, I will for the satisfaction of the Court, shew them it was — impossible to have happen'd, without being observed immediately, as it has been proved to the Court by two Evidences for the prosecution, Captain Kelly and Ensign Van Hamel, that when they Commanded at the Out Posts they sent Monthly Returns to the Governor and duplicates of — them to me agrieable to Orders of the 7th October 1778 here produced and by the Evidence of Serjeant Major Ayres; it appears that from those duplicates the monthly distribution for the Governor was made.

I beg leave further to observe that there never was the least mention made of false returns for four years — and upwards I was under his Command, nor for eighteen Months after the Capture of the Island.

2nd Charge   Improperly employing some of the Forces &c. &c. &c.

To this Charge I think little need be said but to lay before the Court Governor Morris's Order of the 7th October 1778 in which he says as follows, viz.

"A Non Commissioned Officer and twelve Private are to be detached from St. David's /commonly called — Chatteaubellair/ to the Ravine on Colonel Etherington's Land." As also his Order of the 9th October which says;

"The Post at the Ravine on Colonel — Etherington's Land is of course to have Provisions issued from — Chatteaubellair, and the Officer Commanding there to send what Men — he can spare to assist in building the Hutts and clearing round the Post" both which Orders prove that the Men were employed by his — Orders to Establish a new Post for the use of Government on my Land and not cutting Wood by any means for my private benefit.

3rd Charge
  Disobeying several Orders given by said Governor &c. &c. &c.

Though nothing <u>can</u> be proved to the Court, in answer to the first part of the Charge viz. Disobedience of Orders on the 17th September 1778, I say this Charge is so ridiculous that the Order here produced to the Court will shew the absurdity of it without any further Comment.

In answer to the second part of this — Charge, viz., Disobedience of Orders on the 7th October 1778: I say, these Orders were obeyed.

In Answer to the third part of this Charge — viz.,
Disobedience of Orders on the 19th December 1778, I say this is a repetition of the Order of the 17th September 1778 which in no manner concerns me, but the Officer at the Out Posts as will appear to the Court by the Order here produced.

In Answer to the 4th part of this Charge, viz.
Disobedience of Orders on the 1st April 1779 I say this Order was Countermanded by the Order now produced to the — Court.

In answer to the 5th part of this Charge,
viz. —

Disobedience of Orders on the 16th June 1779; I can with solemn truth avow, that I never disobey'd any Order of the 16th June nor has the least proof been given of it.

<u>4th Charge</u>   <u>Neglect of duty and improper behaviour &c. &c. &c.</u>

I say in answer to those Charges they are so vague and inspecific that I am at a loss to know what they mean, however, as such long accounts, Narratives and Opinions, have been delivered to this Court I beg leave to make some observations by which I shall point out; how probably several Evidences for the Prosecution have contradicted each other, nay even how they have contradicted — themselves in the course of their Narrations.

As to Mr. Rellan the first Evidence, he has declar'd on Oath before the Court that it was <u>I</u> who sent the Flag of Truce and gave the Nonsensical Message to Ensign Van Hamel, It has been proved to the Court by said Ensign Van Hamel and all other Evidences for the Prosecution that it was the <u>Governor</u> sent him. He knows there were some Charibbs in Arms, but does not know which part they would have taken; It has been proved to the Court by every other Evidence that they joined the Enemy. He says that after I objected to the Gun to be fired he was ordered out of the Fort and concludes with; "I do not — know what passed afterwards." Notwithstanding this he goes on — relating to the Court an imaginary Conversation which <u>he says</u> he heard between the Governor and me in the Fort the instant following viz. That I had agreed upon Terms of Capitulation &c. &c. &c. — He asserts that the Fort above Kingston is very strong and capable to make a stand at &c. — It has appeared to the Court by Mr. Duncan — Campbell, Mr. George Fraser Sergeant Major Ayres and Sergeant Mc Mullan's Evidence, it is but a Battery en barbette that has neither Ditch nor Palisades; and that all the Troops from the Leeward part of the Island /in his wise opinion/ cou'd have been collected and March'd to Kingston in eight hours; from Chatteaubellair in six. Captain Kelly and Doctor Patrick Connor who lived at Chatteaubellair at that time have proved to the Court that /supposing the Men already collected from — Mornagarou &c. and prepared to March/ it wou'd take from Sun rising to Sun setting, about fourteen hours. From Princes Town to Battery above Kingstown he says is eleven Miles which Soldiers with Arms Accoutrements &c. &c. and a very Mountainous Road /agreeable to his Calculation/ cou'd March in Two hours and a half. He further declares on Oath there were Men on my Land, the day the Enemy Landed, and it has appear'd clear to the Court that he was not there but on the — Battery above Kingston. In short he goes on in the unaccountable — strain, mistaking himself in time, place, distance, and circumstances; knows, sees, hears and thinks things which no body else does; To enumerate all wou'd be very tedious and cause great loss of time to the Court.

I shall finish my remarks on this — Evidence, observing his excessive partiality, to prove which I beg leave to appeal to the Judge Advocate if he has not wrote Letters to him and voluntarily given instructions and Names of Evidences for the Prosecution. There I leave to the Court how far this Man's Testimony may be rely'd on.

On the part of Mr. Duncan Campbell — the second Evidence I shall only observe where <u>he says</u> the Governor told him it was <u>I</u> that ordered the Troops from Hartley's Hill to the Battery; That by the Evidence of Doctor John Connor and Mr. Fraser it appears the <u>Governor</u> gave these Orders.

On the part of Doctor John Connor the 4th Evidence where he seems to intimate, the Troops were a great while in coming to Town, he fully accounts for it when he mentions to the Court that he saw Mr. Phipps come to the Barracks and give me — Orders; What these Orders were, has been already related to the Court by Ensign Van Hamel and Serjeant Major Ayres viz. Not to march — until the Bay of Rothia had been reconnoiter'd.

On the part of Doctor Robert Glasgow the 5th Evidence I must beg leave to make a few remarks; This Gentleman declares to the Court in has Narration of the 16th June 1779 That it was about Two o'clock in the afternoon before the Troops march'd from the Barrack &c. All the other Evidences for the Prosecution have declared it was between <u>ten and eleven o'clock in the forenoon</u> when the Troops march'd down; And it was about <u>four o'clock</u> when I went the first time to the Enemy <u>on my own accord as he heard the Governor declare.</u> Mr. John Bolton says in his Evidence for the Prosecution that it was half past eleven o'clock in the forenoon and declares /as does likewise Doctor John Conner/ Mr. Duncan Campbell, Mr. Fraser and others / that <u>I went by the Governor's Order.</u> Further Doctor Glasgow says; That about four o'clock in the afternoon the Gun was proposed to be fired for the first time. When Mr. Bolton, Doctor John Connor, Mr. Fraser and others declare that the

Capitulation was agreed on between three and four o'clock and the Governor had desired the Inhabitants to go home there being no further use for them.

I believe the Court is by this time — convinced of the Governor's predetermination on the subject of the — Capitulation, as it appears by the Evidence of Mr. Duncan Campbell, that Mr. Malloon his Confidential Secretary had prepared a sketch of a Capitulation like that of Dominique which he shew'd this Evidence at the Government House before ten in the Morning at which time the Enemy were only Landing, And by the Evidence of Doctor John Connor it appears that the Governor had sent Mr. Reynolds one of his Aid de Camps to the Enemy about ten o'clock in the Morning of the 16th of June 1779, with a Letter to the same purport as the Message that Mr. Van Hamel was afterwards sent with but by Doctor Connor's advice he return'd with the Letter to the Government House and declin'd to carry it; By these Circumstances the Governor's intentions may be easily guess'd at.

It seems by the different Narrations of some of the Evidences for the Prosecution as if the Governor had ordered me to call in the Troops from Leeward, which was not the case, and how idle must this appear to the Court if they please to observe, that the Governor effactually Capitulated betwixt three and four o'clock, in the Afternoon of the 16th June 1779, and that had he sent an Express in the Morning on Horseback to call in the Troops from the Leeward Posts; it could not have arrived there before he Capitulated.

As to that part of Mr. Relland's Evidence where he says that he heard the Governor say he had Ordered — me to call in the Troops from Leeward two or three days before the Enemy landed, I have produced to the Court the Governor's Orders of the 16th June 1779 given half an hour before the News was brought of the arrival of the Enemy by which it appears that instead of — adding he diminished the Numbers at the Post of Kingston — /Head Quarters/.

I will not therefore intrude any longer on the patience of the Court by making further observations on — the various misrepresentations and contradictions of some of the Evidences for the Prosecution and for humanity's sake I would rather wish to impute them to their want of Memory /it being near Two Years and a half since the Island was Captured/ than to a Worse Cause. And as so much has been said about — the delay of the Troops in not Marching sooner from the Barracks with other circumstances relative to the 16th of June 1779 I beg leave to relate in a few Words the Transactions of that day viz.

Being at the Government House between nine and ten o'clock in the Morning, news was brought back that the — Enemy were Landing near Calliqua; On which the Governor gave me — orders to go to the Barracks, assemble and March down the Troops to Hartley's Hill, accordingly. I mounted my Horse when the Governor call'd to me and desir'd me to stop a Moment, and in a few Minutes, he came to the Door, and told me that he heard the Enemy had made a second Landing at Rothia Bay, however that I might go up and prepare the Men, and if he heard any more of it he'd let me know, on which I immediately went to the Barracks and gave the necessary Orders for the Men to be got ready which they were, in less than half an hour when Mr. Phipps arrived with Orders for us to remain in the Barracks 'till his return from Rothia, where he was ordered to go and see if — the Enemy was landing to Leeward as the Governor had been informed; as has been proved to the Court by Ensign Van Hamel Serjeant Major Ayres and Serjeant Mc Mullan. In half an hour Mr. Phipps — returned having seen no Enemy to Leeward and we then march'd — agreeable to the Governor's first Order to Hartley's Hill. — On our way — there, near the Church we were overtaken by the Governor, who made a speech to the Men and then called for Ensign Van Hamel, whom he sent off as a Flag of Truce, to learn from the Enemy whether they came with an Hostile intention, If Count D' Estaing Commanded, and to desire — them not to stir, 'till they heard again from him — Mr. Van Hamel then rode off, after which the Troops march'd up Hartley's Hill by a foot path The Governor and I with five or six Townsmen on Horseback rode up — the Hill another way and got up before the Troops arrived; I took that opportunity to go to a rising Ground to take a view of the Enemy, and on my return to the Governor /which was in in a few Minutes/ I was — met by Mr. Reynolds one of his Aid de Camps, who inform'd me that the Governor had in my absence consulted the Gentlemen with him, if that was a proper place to make a stand at, who all agreed it was not, and that the Battery over the Town was the fittest place; On my coming up to the Governor he inform'd me what they had agreed to; I answer'd <u>him</u> — <u>That I was ready to obey his Orders,</u> on which he Commanded the — Men who were just arrived to go down the Hill, which has already been proved by the Evidence of Doctor John Connor and Mr. Fraser for the — Prosecution, upon which we all went to the Battery over the Town and in three quarters of an hour afterwards the Enemy appeared upon Hartley's Hill where they halted a few Minutes and then marched down the Road, at which time the Governor sent Lieutenant Charlton with a party to take possession of the Sugar Work at the Foot of the Hill, and ask why the Flag of Truce was detain'd; if D' Estaing Commanded &c. Lieutenant Charlton return'd and reported that the French Officer told him that D' Estaing did not — Command, but that he had Officers and Men sufficient to take the Island, and if it was not surrendered immediately and without resistance; he cou'd not be answerable for the behaviour of the Troops and Charibbs.

The Governor then address'd himself to the Town's People and said he was sensible of the defenceless state of the Island, and would endeavor to get the best Capitulation he could, On which the Governor order'd Mr. Phipps to go to the French Officer and ask what terms would be granted, and on Mr. Phipps's going off, the Governor — ordered me to follow him, as has been proved to the Court by Mr. Bolton, Doctor John Connor, Mr. Campbell and Mr. Fraser, lest they might not pay him that respect he wish'd, and not being an Officer I told Governor — Morris that it was awkward business to Employ me in; To which he answered "That I was an Officer and spoke French, and therefore a fit person to send, and desired me to make haste and overtake Mr. Phipps which I — accordingly did, and the only Capitulation the Enemy woul'd give was that granted to St. Lucia, which we reported to the Governor, who then called the Town's People into a small Hutt on the Hill near the Battery, with whom he was in Consultation for about half an hour when he came out he call'd to me and desired me to return to the Enemy, and demand the same Terms of Capitulation as granted to Dominica as also for Permission for him to remain on the Island. — I accordingly return'd to the French-Officer, who with difficulty granted his request, and that on condition the Enemy was permitted to take possession of the Sugar Work at the foot of the Hill. — I return'd — and reported this to the Governor who then told the Town's People, he was happy to inform them that he had obtained the same Capitulation as Dominica and that they might now go home in safety as he had — no more occasion for them. The Governor then went to the Court House to prepare the Capitulation which is already proved to the Court by the Evidence of Mr. Bolton.

The Court will be convinced of the Maliginity of the 4th Charge as in reality there was no opportunity of shewing my ardor or Zeal for His Majesty's Service for two very obvious reasons; the first by the Governor's having dispers'd His Majesty's Troops all over the Island, as appears by the monthly distribution of the 1st of June 1779 here produced, and 2ndly by his being personally present with us the — whole day 'till the Capitulation was agreed or as has been proved to the Court by the Evidence for the Prosecution.

It is plain there did not then exist in the Mind of the Governor the least cause of complaint either against the Troops or me; The reason of those Charges brought against me, has arisen since from private resentment occasion'd by my asking him some time after the Capture of the Island, at the <u>request</u> of the Officers and Men, for the Money he had in his hands to a very considerable — amount belonging to three Companies of the 60th Regiment, granted by the Colony for taking up runaway Negroes at St. Vincent's, which on his refusing to pay occasion'd some Words, and ever since that time he has been my declared Enemy; and to convince the Court, of what I have here related in respect of his having no cause of complaint against me — relative to the loss of the Island, until the above mentioned difference; I shall quote a paragraph of Governor Morris's Letter to the Secretary of State of the 22nd June 1779 giving an account of the Capture of it, wrote only six days after the Island was taken when every Circumstance — <u>must</u> have been fresh in his Memory. viz.

"It would be highly unjust to His Majesty's — Officers and Troops and those of the Inhabitants who were able to be collected, not to assure His Majesty which I beg your Lordship to do, — That these shew'd the utmost Alacrity and readiness to endeavor to do by Arms whatever Men were capable of; I had only to regret that their Numbers had not been more considerable, thereby to have given them an opportunity of distinguishing themselves and crowning me with honor, by repulsing this well concerted Attack."

<u>5th Charge</u>   <u>After the Capture of said Island &c. &c. &c.</u>

In answer to this Charge I say; I know not what the Governor means as I was never consulted about the Articles of Capitulation nor was I present either at the making or signing of the Capitulation as appears by the Evidence of Doctor George Young Phisician to the General Hospital Saint Lucia, and at that time Member of the Council of St. Vincent's, and present at the making and signing of the said Capitulation.

I hope Mr. President and Gentlemen of the Court, that you will be fully convinced of the Malice of the several Charges — brought against me, and that I have confuted each of them to your — satisfaction.

I feel myself happy by this public — opportunity of having my Conduct enquired into, and the very high opinion I entertain of the President and Members who compose — this Court-martial induce me to believe they will do ample justice to a Character that private enmity has endeavor'd to Traduce.

And here Gentlemen I close my Defence.

The Defence being closed, The Court proceeded to give Sentence.

The Court having heard, and maturely considered the several Evidences brought in support of the Charges exhibited against the Prisoner, together, with the whole of the Prisoner's Defence, Is of Opinion, That the said Charges are groundless, and malicious, and doth therefore most honorably acquit the Prisoner of the same.

W. Chester, Pres.

C: Smelt

D. Judge Advt.

Horse Guards 16th January 1782

Sir,
    Having had the honor to lay before the — King the Proceedings of a General Court-martial held on the Island of St. Lucia the 5th October last and several subsequent days for the trial of Lieutenant Colonel George Etherington of the 2nd Battalion of the 60th /or Royal American/ Regiment of Foot upon Sundry Articles of — Charge exhibited against him by Valentine Morris Esq. late Governor of the Island of St. Vincent's, viz. —

    1st Giving in False Returns,

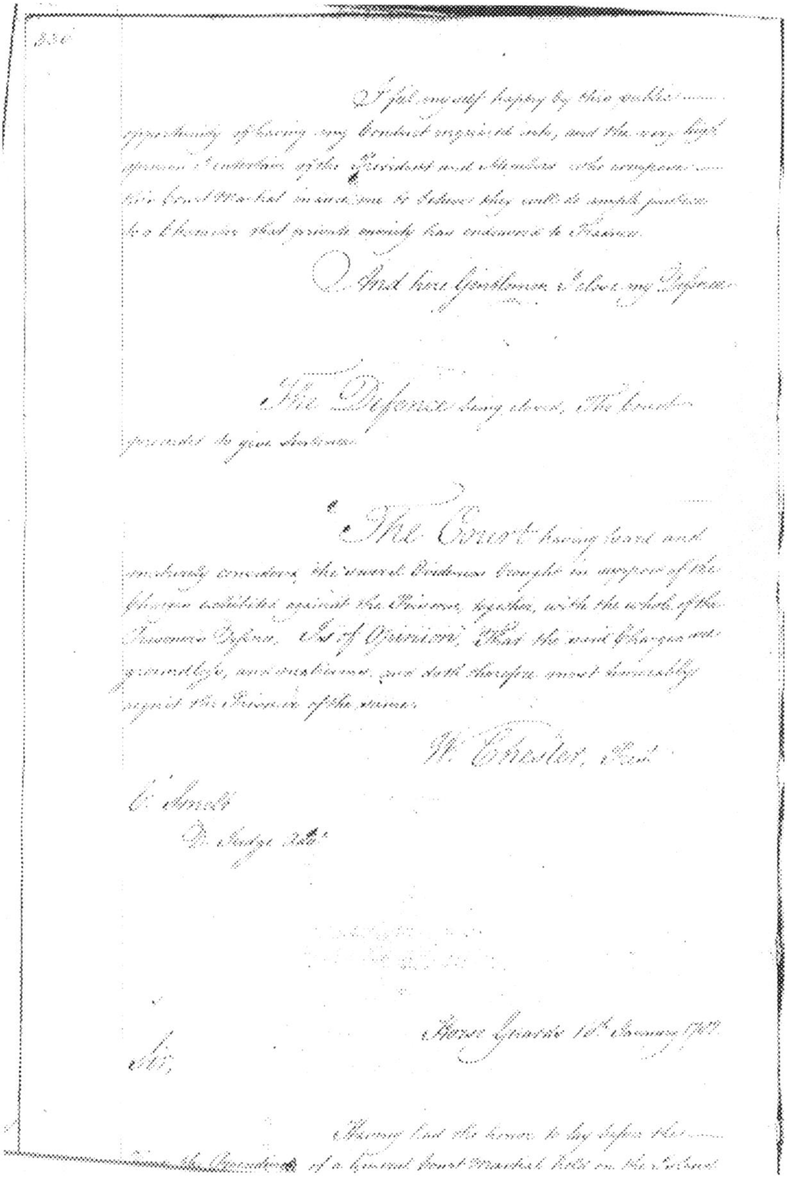
I feel myself happy by this public opportunity of having my Conduct enquired into, and the very high opinion I entertain of the President and Members who compose this Court Martial, induces me to believe they will do ample justice to a Character that private enmity has endeavoured to traduce.

And here Gentlemen I close my Defence.

The Defence being closed, The Court proceeded to give Sentence.

The Court having heard and maturely considered the several Evidences brought in support of the Charges exhibited against the Prisoner, together with the whole of the Prisoner's Defence, Is of Opinion, That the said Charges are groundless, and malicious, and doth therefore most honorably acquit the Prisoner of the same.

W. Chester, Presid.

C. Smith
D. Judge Advt.

Horse Guards 16th January 1782.

Sir,

Having had the honor to lay before the King the Proceedings of a General Court Martial held on the Colonel

Last page of the
1781 Etherington General Court Martial transcript.

Photocopy of original, published with permission, Courtesy: Public Record Office, Kew, Surrey, England (PRO/WO 71/58, ff 271-337).

2nd Improperly employing some of His Majesty's Forces then under his Command in cutting down Wood and doing other — Works upon his own Estate and for his private benefit in the Island of — St. Vincent's,

3rd Disobeying several Orders given by Governor — Morris respecting the distribution of Troops for the safety and defence of the said Island, particularly Orders given on the 17th day of September, 7th day of October and 19th day of December 1778 and on the 1st day of April and 16th day of June 1779,

4th Neglect of duty and improper behaviour in the face of the Enemy,

5th After the Capture of the said Island, advising and endeavoring to induce the Governor to admit of Alterations and — additions in the Articles of Capitulation more advantageous to the — Enemy and derogatory to His Majesty's Honor and Dignity, —

I am commanded to acquaint you, that His — Majesty has been pleased to approve the Opinion of the Court-martial in acquitting the said Lieutenant Colonel Etherington of the several Charges exhibited against him.

His Majesty could however have wished, that Evidence had been laid before the Court by Lieutenant Colonel Etherington in the course of his Defence of some active Endeavors used for the Defence of the Island, or of some judicious measures suggested by him to the Governor, either previous to or at the time of the Descent made by the Enemy.

I have the honor to be,

Sir,

P.S. Inclosed is a —   Your most Obedient Transcript
of the Sentence.   and most humble Servant
            Charles Gould

Brigadier General Christie, or Officer Commanding,
 in Chief His Majesty's Forces in the Leeward and Charibbe Islands &c. &c.   &c.

a Duplicate here of directed to Major General Mathew went by the Packet 6th Febry 1782.

♔ PART III

THE EVIDENCES

(Note: As previously mentioned, this section will examine both Etherington's defense and the various witness testimonies for the prosecution. The "traditional" presentation of Morris's case, aside from those witnesses who are in support of the governor, is based on his own accounts concerning the events of the surrender, as related in Ivor Waters's aforementioned biography of him, specifically pages 66-69. These latter references are preceded by "Morris" and quotations used, where appropriate, to indicate the exact Waters statement. Again, where appropriate, the authors' comments are italicized and indicated by the term "Note.")

With regard to the First Charge – Giving in False Returns;

Prosecution – The only witnesses who answered directly to this charge were Mr. Rellan, as a deponent, Serjeant Major Ayres and Ensign Van Hamel. "The Deponent produced to the Court a Return of a Detachment of the British Troops at Fort Guilford, dated 14 April 1779, which consisted of 2 Subs, 2 Serjeants, 2 Drummers, and 20 Rank and File, which he declared were "more than was at any other Post, in the Charaibbe Country, and that there was <u>no addition</u> made afterwards."

Serjeant Major Ayres and Ensign Van Hamel both refuted the charge as they were directly involved in the handling of them.

Etherington – He stated, to this charge, "no thing has been proved." He put forth that it was impossible for this to have happened without being observed immediately, as the officers at the outposts sent monthly returns to the governor and duplicates of them to himself, this being consistent with the orders of 7 October 1778.

(Note: Additionally, quite separate from the court-martial, but relating to this charge, in an exchange of letters in 1777, between Captain Morse, Commanding Engineer and Senior Officer for the

Ceded Islands, and Lord Barrington, Secretary at War. The captain complained of Etherington that he did not send him returns and status reports, directly, as he thought he should do, he being the senior officer; in fact, he said, he refused utterly! Lord Barrington responded that Etherington had been sending the returns and reports directly to the governor or lieutenant-governor on the Island of St. Vincent's and it was quite proper for him to do so.)

With regard to the Second Charge – Improperly employing some of the Forces then under His Command, in cutting down wood and doing other works upon his own Estate and for His Private Benefit in the said Island of St. Vincent's.

Seven of the thirteen witnesses gave evidences relating to this charge and they all agreed that there were soldiers on Etherington's estate. Four of the witnesses, Serjeant Major Ayres, Ensign Van Hamel, Captain Kelly and Doctor Patrick Connor, all stated that the purpose for the soldiers being there was to construct a post; Ensign Van Hamel and Captain Kelly both further testified that the fort (battery), under construction, was by the order of the governor, Captain Kelly adding that it was a "written order."

Of the remainder of the witnesses, Mr. Rellan was never queried regarding the purpose. Mr. Campbell said that he never heard there was to be a post and that he <u>believed</u> that the ongoing work was for Etherington's benefit. Mr. Wilkie said that he hadn't heard there was to be a post but that the *situation* was proper for such.

As to the number of soldiers at work on the land, Mr. Rellan said that he <u>heard</u> there were 60 to 70 but saw only 8 to 10; Mr. Campbell said he saw above ten; Mr. Wilkie said that a corporal at the site said there were 60 but that he saw only 20 to 25; Doctor Patrick Connor said he saw 20 to 30; Captain Kelly said that the *base number* was 13 but that it varied; Serjeant Major Ayers and Ensign Van Hamel were not ask'd about the number.

As to whether the soldiers working on the estate were properly armed and appointed: Mr. Rellan said some were and some not; Doctor Patrick Connor said by what he saw of their arms, they were not; the remainder of the witnesses were not asked. It is to be recalled, however, that there was a lack of arms available on the island.

As to whether the soldiers were engaged in cutting wood, clearing, and burning: Mr. Campbell, Mr. Rellan and Doctor Patrick Connor all testified that they had witnessed such activity; the remainder of the witnesses were not asked.

Captain Kelly, giving evidence with regard to the existence of written orders, testified that there were and the Fort Adjutant signed them. He continued that in October of 1778 he was detached to Chateaubellair and that "a Serjeant and 12 Men were Ordered from his Post, by Governor Morris, to the Colonel's Land, and that in addition, he was also Ordered to assist those Men with any additional that might be required for the purpose of clearing the Ground and building Hutts for the Men, as a Battery was intended to be built there."

Etherington – He referred the Court to the Captain Kelly's testimony regarding Written Orders from the governor and read into the transcript additional information from those orders, as follows: "The Post at the Ravine on Colonel Etherington's Land is of course to have Provisions issued from Chateaubellair, and the Officer Commanding there is to send what Men he can spare to assist the building of Hutts and clearing around the Post." He concluded from the two orders "it is proven that the Men employed there was for the purpose of establishing a new Post for the use of the Government on His Land and not cutting wood by any means for his private benefit."

With regard to the Third Charge – Disobeying Several Orders given by said Governor, respecting the Distribution of Troops for the Safety and Defense of said Island, particularly Orders given on the 17th day of September, 7th day of October and 19th day of December, 1778, and 1st April and 16th day of June, 1779;

Serjeant Major Ayres responded to the charge that he never heard of any instance and he was the only Witness to respond directly to it.

Etherington – He offered to the Court a production of documents with regard to the Orders in question and commented on them as follows: The 19th December 1778 Order was a repetition of 17th September 1778 and concerned him not directly but rather the Officers at the Out Posts and they must be questioned regarding that; 1st April 1779 was countermanded by a subsequent Order that he gave the Court in Evidence. As to the disobedience of Order on the 16th June 1779 he emphatically denied the accusation, entirely.

With regard to the Fourth Charge – Neglect of Duty and with Improper Behaviour in the Face of the Enemy;

Only five witnesses responded directly to the charge; four of the five were military, Serjeant Major Ayres, Serjeant McMullan, Ensign Van Hamel, and Captain Kelly; they all emphatically testified that there had been no instances as far as they knew. Mr. Campbell *dodged a direct response* and offered that it was Governor Morris who had failed — he said the governor told him that he was aware of the French landing several days prior and he asked him, "why he was not more forward in his preparations to receive them?" Mr. Rellan said that the governor told him that he had notice four or five days before the French attacked the island. When he was asked what steps the governor took in view of the "intelligence," he said that the governor had sent for Colonel Etherington and told him to take proper steps to defend the island; and a day or two later he asked him (Etherington) why the men had not come in from his estate as he expected the French to land at any hour. Mr. Rellan said that the colonel, to this, said to the governor "not to be 'uneasy' as the men would be up time enough."

None of the following witnesses, Doctor John Conner, Mr. Rellan, Mr. Richardson, Mr. Campbell, Serjeant Major Ayres, Serjeant McMullan, Ensign Van Hamel, &c. &c. testified that the colonel appeared reluctant to engage the enemy nor did they know of any of the troops or officers voicing such concerns. There were a few *uninspired attempts* to suggest that was the case but they soon modified to 'perhaps he could have been more aggressive.'

Mr. Campbell added, with regard to this charge, an "interesting occurrence" that once again doesn't make to the point of the charge but does offer a condemnation of the governor. "Shortly after the French Landed, he was at the Governor's House, and while there, Mr. Mallon expressed a desire to speak with him after he (Campbell) had wondered aloud, 'Why if Governor Morris knew in advance of the French Attack did he not make preparations for it?' At this time, Mr. Mallon, who was a person in the confidence of the Governor, took me aside, and said that he had been preparing something in the form of a Capitulation, which he had chiefly taken from the Dominica one, which he had in his pocket. He desired me to look over what he had wrote. I told him that it wou'd be time enough when it was determined to give up the Island." He continued that, at that, he went to the governor to determine if he meant to make any defense and he (the governor) claimed that it was his intention. When later asked if he thought the governor would have attempted to defend the island had the colonel supported him he said he didn't think so because he didn't attempt to collect the inhabitants nor did he even attempt to carry the two field pieces near his house to the entrenchments. Campbell had made this suggestion, and volunteered to do; and to that suggestion and offer, he had gotten no response. When asked about the troops to Leeward, he opinioned that they could have arrived by the morning of the 17th had the governor ordered them or if the colonel had brought them without orders, which he said he thought would have been proper. To this last, Doctor John Connor concurred and added that if the troops had arrived, the combined force could have defeated the French, there being 60 British Regulars and 30 inhabitants. Mr. Rellan, on the other hand, flatly stated that the governor was anxious to engage the enemy.

Doctor Glasgow offered that it was the governor's responsibility to defend the island and that had the colonel offered to take command, the governor would have accepted.

Etherington – He offers a very lengthy denial where he addresses each witness's testimony. He concluded, "I will not therefore intrude any longer on the patience of the Court by making further observation on the various misrepresentations and contradictions of some of the Evidences for the Prosecution and for humanity's sake I would rather wish to impute them to their want of memory /it being near two years and a half since the Island was Captured/ than to a worse cause."

With regard to the Fifth Charge – After the Capture of the said Island by Advising and Endeavouring to Induce the Governor to admit Alterations and Additions in the Articles of Capitulation more Advantageous to the Enemy and Derogatory to His Majesty's Honour and Dignity.

There were no direct responses to this charge by any of the prosecution witnesses.

Etherington – He made the claim that he was never consulted about the Articles of Capitulation nor was he present either at their making or their signing. He then brought forward the only witness for his defense, Doctor George Young, previously a member of the council in St. Vincent's; he witnessed that the colonel was not present at either the making or the signing.

The Events of 16th June 1779 – The French Landing of Troops

Morris (as per Waters) – "A messenger came from the Windward side of the island, on horseback, *at full speed*, from the Carib

Country, to tell Governor Morris that three vessels, two of about 20 Guns and the other larger, were coming down the coast towards Kingstown."

(Note: The rider's route from the Carib Country, would have begun in the area of Grand Sable, it being located about two thirds of the way up the Windward side, north of Kingstown. He could only taken the High Road south along the coast, as that was the only road into that area. Once reaching the Jambou River (Yambou River), he would have been able to cut across the Island to Kingstown, as the road at that point swings overland to the west. The initial French landing, thought to have been at Byrea Beach, is located about a mile to the south of Grand Sable. One would surmise that the rider must been to the south of Byrea Beach when he saw the three ships – as if he had been north of that, he would either have seen four ships or the French troops landing. The fact that the ships were English-built, flying no colors or English colors, the accounts vary, would not have prompted such haste on the rider's part – he had to believe that they were the enemy. Oddly, there was a battery on top of Dorchester Hill at that time, and one would expect a 'spotter' there would be the one to announce the approach of ships from the Windward, usually indicated with the raising of a signal flag; however, it may not have been in existence at this time. One last point, in order to reach to governor prior to the landing, the 'rider' would have to have ridden through the night owing to the distance, probably about 15 miles or better, and that being the case, he couldn't have been aware of such details as the number of cannon.)

Mr. Rellan when asked if there had been time for all the troops, or any part of them, to have joined the colonel from the time the alarm was sounded, evaded the question, simply stating, "...there was no alarm until the enemy landed."

(Note: The "intelligence" that three armed vessels were sailing down the Windward side, heading toward Kingstown, should have prompted the governor to cause the alarm to be sounded especially, as he later claimed, that "he was expecting the Enemy at any moment." This would have been the usual route for ships coming from the French islands.)

Morris – "In fact, the three Sloops of War appeared at about 9:00 o'clock in the morning of the 16th of June, 1779, off Calliqua, two anchoring in Young's Bay *(directly off Calliqua)* and the other in

Warrawarrou Bay" *(a bay just to the west, about a mile distant.)* They flew no colors and the colonists assumed them to be "merchant-men" and declined to raise the alarm.

(Note: Young's Bay and Warrawarrou Bay [Greathead's Bay or Crooke's Bay] essentially form one contiguous bay delineated only by a 'bit of a headland' and a small island, Young's Island. Likely, though separated, all three ships were in sight of each other. The presence of one ship in Warrawarrou Bay is a bit of a mystery in that the surrounding hills are quite high and have batteries mounted atop them. Should the ship have been fired upon, it could not have elevated its guns sufficiently to have returned fire; its very location put it at risk. However, the French may have been aware that the keys 'were missing' from Wilkies Battery and that the Battery on Mr. Hartley's Hill [Sion Hill] wasn't manned.)

Morris – The "Ships were British-built" and that, coupled with the fact that the colonists were expecting "merchant-men" from Antigua to come to pick up sugar for England, caused their confusion. In their anxiety to make the first shipment for the year, the colonists even went so far as to prevent a gunner on Hyde's Point Battery (Ratho Mill Point) from sounding an alarm.

(Note: As it was evident to the 'rider' that they were the enemy or at the very least ships of war, so should it have been just as obvious to the inhabitants. These ships, heavily armed were not 'merchant-men' and the presence of one anchored off in Warrawarrou Bay would further suggest that as there were no loading facilities there.)

(Note: Sugar cane is cut beginning in the spring months and cutting and processing completed by August or September, that being the beginning of the hurricane season. Being June, it is doubtful that this would have been the 'first sugar' to ship in the year.)

Morris – "Mr. Collins, who had strenuously opposed calling out the militia, was so convinced that they (the Ships) were British that he went on board and was taken Prisoner."

Morris – By now, De La Roche and his troops had control of all of the Windward side of St. Vincent's, encountering no resistance. Upon his landing at Calliaqua, Mons. Le Chevallier Du Rumain, was greeted by De La Roche and his troops. Du Rumain formed up some troops on Sir William Young's Hill (estate) and marched for Kingstown, some 500 strong.

(Note: When the first of the French landed at Byrea Beach, they marched to Colonaire and attacked the fort. Lieut. Gordon and James Glasgow gathered up some troops and tried to defend as best they could, but being outnumbered two to one, they soon were overwhelmed. As previously noted, this incident is apparently the only 'resistance' they encountered.)

Doctor John Connor estimated the enemy force at 120 to 130 Regulars and about 250 others of different colors; Mr. Bolton estimated their strength at about 300, Mulattoes &c.; Sergeant Major Ayres said he saw 300 to 400; Doctor Glasgow said he <u>heard</u> there were 250 besides the Charaibs; Mr. Rellan, to the best of his judgment, saw about 350, and added that some were Regulars, he knew not how many, and some were Volunteers composed of White People, Negroes, and Mulattoes; when Mr. Rellan was asked about the presence of Charaibs, he said he <u>heard</u> it was so but knew not if they would have taken part.

Morris – William Crooke, "who had refused to allow entrenchment to be made near his Bay (Warrawarrow Bay), was plundered and stripped nearly naked."

(Note: Mr. Crooke owned several properties, singularly, and some jointly, with Mr. Greathead. From the description of the location, likely the Plantation being referenced is the one at Arno's Vale, an area more-or-less in the 'heart' of the Warrawarrou Bay.)

Mr. Rellan testified that it took the French force about two hours to reach Mr. Crooke's sugar-works after they landed. When asked if they had landed any cannon, he replied that he had never <u>heard</u> of any.

Immediately after the French landing, the first orders with regard to defense and the preparation time taken to respond to them --

Doctor Glasgow gave evidence that he saw the French landing, and judged them to be so on account of their dress. He gave this news to Doctor John Connor and Mr. Cunningham (master of a "merchant-man"), whom he met. They agreed that Doctor Glasgow would ride to Government House to speak with the governor and that Mr. Cunningham and Doctor John Connor would go to town to warn the inhabitants and then ride on, to speak with the colonel, where he was, at the barracks on Berkshire Hill (later the site of 19th-century Fort Charlotte).

Doctor Glasgow, when he arrived at Government House saw the governor and Colonel Etherington together, and he told them of the French landing at Sir William Young's Bay. Upon learning this, the governor, he said, told Colonel Etherington to "go immediately to the Barracks and March the Men down to make the best defense possible and to send off an 'Express' to Captain Kelly to use every expedition to bring the Men down from Chateau Bellair." He went on to say that upon being given his orders, the colonel went away and Doctor Glasgow then retired to his house to await the arrival of the troops from the barracks. Upon examination, he said he did not know if the "express" had been sent but that the orders were given to Colonel Etherington to do so at 10:00 to 11:00 o'clock in the morning. He also added, when questioned, that he did not recollect that there were others present at the time, just himself.

Etherington – He stated that <u>he was at Government House</u> but between 9:00 and 10:00 o'clock in the morning and it was there that he got the news that the enemy were landing at Calliaqua, and that the governor <u>did give him orders</u> to go to the barracks and assemble the men and <u>march down the troops to Hartley's Hill</u> (Sion Hill); he mentioned nothing about being ordered to send an "Express" to Captain Kelly. Additionally, he added that as he was about to depart, the governor called him back and advised him that he had heard of a *second landing* at Rothia Bay (Ottley's Bay) and that he would pass along further information as he learned more of it. Serjeant Major Ayres added to the story that he had heard a *rumor* of the enemy landing, between 9:00 and 10:00 o'clock in the morning, and that, the colonel not being present (in the barracks) at the time, he ordered the troops to get ready. Serjeant McMullan testified that the troops were under arms between 10:00 and 11:00 o'clock in the morning; Mr. Fraser, being at the barracks at that time, agreed.

Doctor Patrick Connor testified that an "Express," on horseback, might reach Chateaubellair from Kingstown in five hours — Etherington did not dispute the estimate. Captain Kelly offered his view, that the ride, at night, would likely take seven hours.

Captain Kelly stated that he learned of the French landing at about 12:00 o'clock in the morning, from Doctor Patrick Connor, who was at Chateaubellair. Doctor Patrick Connor said that he had learned of the landing about 9:00 or 10:00 in the morning on the 16th.

(Note: Doctor Patrick Connor did not say how he came by this information or why it took him 2 to 3 hours to pass it along to Captain Kelly; nor was he asked. Allowing that the event began at 9:00 o'clock in the morning, even by "express," he could not have learned of it until 2:00 o'clock in the afternoon.)

Captain Kelly continued testifying as to the situation of the troops at Chateaubellair. He said "there were 49 troops and 25 on the Colonel's land and that as soon as he learned of the French landing he recalled those from the Colonel's Estate, which was only two miles to the north." He also stated "that while he didn't receive an 'Express' from the Colonel, he did receive a letter at about 10:00 or 11:00 o'clock in the morning of the 16th, advising him to have his Detachment in readiness to March at a moment's warning." When asked "how long it would have taken to March the troops to Town, he said that with the 'greatest effort' that it would have taken from sun rising to sun down. It was suggested to Captain Kelly that he and his Troops might have been able to reached Kingstown more quickly if they had gone by boat rather than overland." To this he replied that he wouldn't have been able to procure boats. He opinioned that the entire force of the Island, other than his own, could have joined within 8 hours, except those in the Carib Country. Mr. Rellan offered that there were upwards of 100 Troops in the Carib Country, of the 200 to 300 total. When Captain Kelly was asked, "cou'd the Troops (at Kingstown) not have retired and joined those in the Country?" — he answered "Yes!"

(Note: Presumably the "letter" from the colonel was sent prior to the French landing, at least the day earlier, for it to have reached by 10:00 to 11:00 o'clock the morning of the 16th. The "letter" may have been sent in response to the governor advising him that an eemy attack on the island was imminent.)

(Note: The proposal that the troops in Kingstown could have retried and joined those at Chateaubellair was never further pursued.)

Morris (as per prosecution witness noted below) – The keys to Wilkie's Battery were found to be missing but still no alarm was given.

(Note: Wilkie's Battery was located on a small headland that reaches only a little way out into Warrawarrou Bay; it is situated on the east side, quite near Mr. Crooke's Estate, which is less that a half mile distant.)

Mr. Campbell had met up with Mr. Fraser, and the two of them determined that they would fire the Guns in the Battery (presumably Wilkie's Battery). "They found the Guns unloaded and then went and had to break down the door to the Gunner's house; there, they discovered no cartridges or powder. At that moment, a Negro came by and told them that the French were marching towards them. They hastened out, mounted their horses, and were caused to take a 'precipitous route' towards Town as the Enemy had gotten between them and the Main Road."

Morris – Governor Morris, "with forty-three of forty-four troops" did what he could by positioning himself, and some troops, along with one or two Cannon, on Sion Hill (Mr. Hartley's Hill). The French estimated their (the British) number at between sixty and eighty, no more. Morris caused entrenchments to be thrown up in defense, while they awaited the arrival of Lieutenant-Colonel Etherington and his troops from the Leeward side.

Mr. Rellan, with regard to the previous Hartley's Hill (Sion Hill) incident, outlined just above, was asked a battery of questions relating specifically to it. His responses were that "there were forty three Regular British Troops and about thirty Inhabitants and that they could have defended until the Troops under the Command of Captain Kelly, arrived from Leeward where they were Posted at Chateaubellair (Richmond Town), it being only sixteen or seventeen miles distant." *(Note: The actual distance is 21 miles.)* He estimated that "it would have taken them about six hours and that the Troops from Prince's Town (Barrowallie) could have arrived in about two and a half, it being only eleven miles *(Note: The actual distance is 12 miles.)*, however, none of them arrived at the Fort on the 16th." He further offered that "the Enemy could not have prevented them from joining nor could some of the others, only those in the Carib Country were thus prevented."

(Note: Etherington's Estate at Morne Ronde was actually 24 miles distant.)

According to Mr. Campbell's testimony, he and Mr. Fraser took a route up Hartley's Hill (Sion Hill) on their way to town, having just narrowly escaped the enemy while at Wilkie's Battery. There they met Mr. Lees, the military engineer, with a few Negroes, at the entrenchments on the top. When asked what arrangements the governor and Colonel Etherington had made for defense, he said that they had made none and his opinion was that they did not plan to. He said he had been sent by the governor and told to wait to receive the King's troops. At that, they departed and traveled to Government House to speak with the governor. On their way, they met Doctor John Connor who accompanied them part way, and then continued on, to the barracks on Berkshire Hill (Fort Charlotte), to acquaint the colonel with the situation.

Doctor John Connor described the barracks on Berkshire Hill (Fort Charlotte site) as being surrounded by a stone wall, having two field pieces therein. He added that he did not think it to be a very defensible position and that the battery behind the town, with the two 18 pounders, was the better choice.

When Doctor John Connor arrived at the barracks, according to his testimony, he asked the colonel if he had heard of the enemy's landing, or if he had received orders, in consequence, from the governor. The colonel said that he had orders to occupy the trenches. The doctor then posed a barrage of questions, regarding the actions that the colonel had taken, to which he denied a response. The doctor then moved to the gallery and still saw no troops readying themselves; immediately he sought out the colonel once again to find out what was causing the delay. Etherington responded stating that he did not understand the governor's orders 'to occupy the trenches' as he knew not which that he meant. He went on to say that his intention was to remain at the barracks and defend them. Upon being challenged by the doctor to undertake the defense of the island, he reported that Colonel Etherington flatly refused, indicating that it was the governor's responsibility.

Etherington – He testified that he had learned of the enemy's landing and was ordered by the governor to assemble the troops and march them to Hartley's Hill (Sion Hill); however, at that time, he was also put on notice, by the governor, that there might have been a *second landing* at Rothia Bay (Ottley's Bay). Serjeant Major Ayres testified that as soon as the colonel returned to the barracks, he urged that the men prepare "in all haste." Etherington further testified that within a half hour of his return to the barracks, Mr. Phipps, aid de camp to the governor, rode up and advised him to delay, until his return. Upon Mr. Phipps' return, some time later, he advised that there had been no *second landing* and at that, the Order was given to March the Troops to Mr. Hartley's Hill (Sion Hill). Serjeant Major Ayres testified that the Troops were somewhat further delayed from immediately marching, having to take shelter from a heavy downpour.

(Note: From the testimony of Doctor Glasgow we learn that the Governor and the Colonel were together early in the morning of the 16th and that the Doctor was the first on the scene to impart the news to them of the Enemy's landing and Etherington is in agreement with this. That at that time, Governor Morris, specifically told him to assemble the Troops and <u>*March them to Hartley's Hill*</u> *(Sion Hill) is also something else they are in agreement upon. That being the case, Doctor John Conner's testimony, concerning the Colonel being determined to remain at the Barracks because he didn't know which entrenchments to March the Men to &c., seems to be in question. There are other minor conflicting 'bits and pieces', and some omissions, however, they aren't terribly important.)*

Ensign Van Hamel testified that at about 9:00 in the morning, on the 16th, he was in the town when he heard about he enemy landing. Immediately, he said, he made his way to the barracks and found the soldiers employed in filling their pouches with ammunition and fixing their flints, &c., apparently at the behest of Serjeant Major Ayres. Upon being further questioned, Ensign Van Hamel stated that the men were properly prepared with sufficient ammunition — "They had plenty, I saw them provided myself." Serjeant McMullan also testified that the men were properly provided with ammunition, "I took the Cartridges out of the Store and delivered plenty to each Man." Whilst the men were busy about this, Mr. Phipps, aid de camp to Governor Morris, came up to Colonel Etherington with orders, that the troops were not to march until he inspected Rothia Bay (Ottley's Bay) to see if a *second French landing* had taken place, as rumored. "In about an half hour," he returned saying that there were none; and at that, the troops "fell-in," and began their march to town. Mr. Fraser, who had previously come to the barracks, testified that the troops were under arms by 11:00 o'clock in the morning and this is in agreement with the testimony given by Serjeant Major Ayres.

After speaking with the colonel, Doctor John Connor testified that he "departed the barracks and was headed towards Government House when he met the governor, about half way." He advised the governor of the colonel's "confusion" and after some discussion they agreed that he must be delivered written orders, immediately. Also they agreed that an "express" must be gotten off right away to Admiral Byron appraising him of the situation and additionally that the gun at the battery at Akers must be spiked. They were in agreement that they had to do what they could, to *hold out*, "'till they cou'd be relieved by General Grant" (presumably in Barbados). Doctor John Connor then went to town, but found few people, as the greater part had gone for their arms. Upon seeing this, he then proceeded to retrace his steps to the barracks, once again. Upon arriving, he sought out the colonel and advised him of his conversation with the governor and told him that the governor had complained of his "not possessing the trenches according to his Orders." At that moment, Mr. Phipps arrived, and delivered the colonel written orders. The doctor further stated that "Etherington, at that time, said that he would go and see the governor, and with that, the Doctor departed towards Town and this time along the way, he met Mr. Reynolds, another Aid de Camp to the Governor; he was carrying in his hand a paper written in French, to be delivered to the French Commandant." He had been ordered to ascertain why he was in St. Vincent's. "Blockhead" said the doctor, of the governor, and then he advised Reynolds that "if he attempted to penetrate the French Lines he'd likely be shot as a Spy; at that, Reynolds turned and went back to the Governor."

About that same time, after stopping to report to the governor, Mr. Fraser was making his way to the barracks when he met Colonel Etherington on the road, headed presumably, to visit the governor. Fraser continued to the barracks and gave evidence that when he arrived he noted the British troops under arms, for the first time, about 11:00 o'clock in the morning.

About the number of troops at the fort (barracks), Mr. Rellan testified that there were forty-two but that he knew not how the rest of the troops were deployed throughout the island, but that there were about 200. He said that the officers present at the barracks were "Captain Etherington, William Wheatly, William Charlton, Lieutenant Walker and Lieutenant Barker."

Doctor Glasgow, having waited at his house for an hour and a half, expecting the troops to appear from the barracks, returned to Government House to ascertain the reason for the delay. Soon after, Mr. Phipps arrived with the news that there was no enemy landing to Leeward and that the colonel had sent with him a message to know "where the Men were to be march'd to."

(Note: Recall that Etherington had previously agreed that the governor told him to march the men to Hartley's Hill (Sion Hill) and Mr. Rellan also gave evidence that he heard Governor Morris /in company/ order Etherington to march from the barracks to Hartley's Hill.)

Mr. Campbell testified that shortly after Colonel Etherington rode up and inquired of the governor to which entrenchments he was to march, the governor said, "Did I not Order you two hours ago to March the King's Troops to the entrenchments?"   In response, Etherington raised the point that he was delayed, having to wait on Mr. Phipps to learn if the enemy had landed to Leeward at Ottley's Bay (Bay of Rothia) and *suggested* that he still didn't have any information regarding it. He then rode off saying, "I warrant that the King's Troops will be in Time to do their Duty."

(Note: This last is inconsistent with Etherington's testimony in that he stated that Mr. Phipps had come to the barracks and advised them that there was no Leeward landing.)

Mr. Richardson, also at Government House when all this was going on, stated, "At this moment, Colonel Etherington came riding up, and the Governor said, 'for God's sake, get your Men, and go up to the intrenchments.' He said Etherington immediately rode off."

(Note: This whole series of testimony is quite "confused" and "conflicting" and doesn't seem to have any purpose to it.   The prosecutor didn't make any effort to resolve the differences in the testimony of his witnesses, and oddly, neither did the Court. However, in deciphering its entirety, the discrepancies do not have any real significance and the testimonies inevitably support Etherington's contentions.)

Other Conversations at Government House
(re: Morris's claim that Etherington took one, two hours to deploy the troops)

Morris – "Lieutenant-Colonel Etherington took two hours to give the Orders to March, and Morris said, '.. the Act of Starting took another half hour.'"

Mr. Rellan testified that he heard Governor Morris say /in company/ that he had ordered the King's troops, and such of the inhabitants as could be collected, to the trenches; and that he had ordered Colonel Etherington, two hours ago, to march to them also, and he was surprised what had detained him. Mr. Campbell made a similar question to the governor and he also was told that the colonel had been ordered to march over two hours prior. Mr. Richardson also volunteered that he and others were told by the governor that he had sent two or three messages to the colonel to muster the men but that he saw no appearance of any movement.

Doctor Glasgow, in conversation with Mr. Phipps and the governor, was present when the colonel rode up and inquired, "where the Troops were to be March'd to." Mr. Campbell was likewise present and heard the colonel ask, "where the Troops were to be March'd to" — additionally, under questioning, he added that he had heard nothing regarding the French landing to Leeward.

The Troops are marched from the Barracks to Town and Ensign Van Hamel is sent out to the Enemy with a Flag of Truce

Ensign Van Hamel, in testimony, stated that "the Troops would have been march'd sooner if they had not been Order'd to wait for Mr. Phipps' return from reconnoitering the Bay of Rothia (Ottley's Bay)"; and as to the time the March began, he stated that it was "a little after 10:00 o'clock in the morning."

Mr. Glasgow testified that the colonel had "gotten his Orders to March between 10:00 and 11:00 o'clock in the morning" and that it was about 2:00 o'clock in the afternoon when he proceeded.

Doctor John Connor testified, "In a short time afterwards, I met the Colonel coming up from Government House, who told me the Troops were Ordered to the Hill (Hartley's Hill, Sion Hill), and I proceeded with the Colonel and joined the Troops. The Governor soon came up and I recommended to him to Beat to Arms, and the Inhabitants would join him when they knew that any real thing was intended. Upon which the drums Beat to Arms and several of the Inhabitants joined us, but the Governor did not permit them to join the Troops, but Ordered them to a Fort above the Town (Dorchester Hill)."

Mr. Campbell added that he "previously had departed the Barracks and gone to Town and it was not until nearly and hour later that he heard 'the musick of the 60th Regiment' coming into Town. He mounted his horse and took a Fuzee in his hand and went and joined them near the Custom House." His testimony agreed in substance with that offered by Doctor John Connor regarding the inhabitants. In addition, he said he asked the governor if he had sent anybody to give him information of the situation and advances of the Enemy, and when the Governor acknowledged he had not, Campbell went on to Mr. Crooke's plantation.

Ensign Van Hamel's testimony regarding the march is that he had, of course, "joined the Troops as they departed the Barracks and March'd to Town." When they were near the church, they were overtaken by the governor who delivered a "pompous speech" and then took command. In a little while after, the governor called and ordered the ensign to go, as a flag of truce, to the enemy, and to ask them whether they came with hostile intentions, and to determine who commanded, and to desire them not to advance any further 'till they heard again from him. The ensign hesitated some time and the governor noticing that, shot out, "Sir, it is my Positive Orders you go off immediately and take a Drummer with you!" The message that he was to deliver was to the same purpose as that previously sent with Mr. Reynolds. Doctor Glasgow, and Mr. Fraser's evidences, regarding the matter, were in agreement with the ensign's testimony. The ensign continued, that having obtained horses for himself and the drummer, they departed towards Calliaqua. Serjeant Major Ayres added that when the ensign and drummer rode off, the governor came to the front of the troops and "March'd with them through the Town of Kingstown"…and nearing Hartley's Hill (Sion Hill) the governor "Ordered the Troops to ascend by a Bye Road and the Governor and others went up the High Road." In response to a question put by the colonel, Mr. Richardson testified that about 8 or 10 inhabitants accompanied he and the governor.

Morris – "Upon Etherington's arrival, Morris, Etherington, and a few others, all on horseback, rode up the Hill (Hartley's Hill, Sion Hill) and when they reached the top they saw the Enemy less than a half-mile away."

Morris – "The French Troops were put to rest at noon and Mons. De Canonge was sent to reconnoiter; about fifteen minutes later, he returned with a Drummer and an English Ensign Van Hamel, who said that the Governor had sent him to ascertain what he (Du Rumain) was doing on the Island. Du Rumain was taken aback at the question and Ordered Van Hamel to be sent to the rear and kept under observation."

Mr. Campbell, on his way to Mr. Crooke's plantation, overtook Ensign Van Hamel and the drummer. The ensign was afoot, as he had fallen from his horse, that caused by a broken girth of his saddle. Mr. Campbell ascertained his mission and offered his horse after commenting on how ridiculous the message was. The ensign and the drummer rode off and Mr. Campbell continued on foot to a rising ground that over looked the sugar works where the French troops had halted. He commented, "I had not long been there, before they began their March, and had a very distinct view of them; one third of them had not cartouche boxes, and seem'd to be very ill Arm'd. I reckoned them as near as I cou'd, and imagined their number to be about two hundred and sixty of all kinds, Troops, Volunteers, Mulattoes, &c. I took up my flintlock, which I had laid by, and made the best of my way towards the intrenchments."

Ensign Van Hamel continued his testimony, "I fell in a little time, after meeting Mr. Campbell, with a Reconnoitering Party consisting of an Officer /whose name I learn'd afterwards was Canonge/ and about twenty Men, who conducted me to the Troops which were laying on their Arms near the Negroe Houses of said Mr. Crooke's Estate, about two miles from Town. I delivered my message to the Commanding Officer (Du Rumain), to which he ans'd with a smile, that he came to subdue the Island, under the Obedience of His Most Christian Majesty and that his name was Frolong Du Rumain, &c. Fully satisfied as to the truth of his reply /after casting my eye over the Troops/ I mounted my horse again, but as I was going back I was stop'd by Mons. Canonge who desired me to return." Mons. Frolong Du Rumain advised Mons. "Canonge not to let me go back to Kingstown, which he approved of. I was then Ordered to alight, as was likewise the Drummer, to which I objected in vain by saying it was against the Custom of War to detain a Flag of Truce, and I was given in charge of the grenadiers and march'd with them in front of the Troops. They moved on, very slowly, with the Reconnoitering Party's advance, and halted near the summit of Mr. Hartley's Hill (Sion Hill). They were joined in a short time by about 500 Charaibbs, Arm'd with Fuzee and Cutlass." Serjeant Major Ayres, had, in separate testimony, estimated about four hundred immediately with the French, and some small parties upon the neighboring hills. Mr. Rellan advanced that he "did not see the Ensign again 'till after the Island Surrendered."

The Advance of the British Troops to
Mr. Hartley's Hill (Sion Hill)

Doctor Anderson, second curator of the Botanic Garden, described Mr. Hartley's Hill (Sion Hill) — "The Sion Hill (Mr. Hartley's Hill) is a small but flat prominence on a ridge that begins at Bluff Point,

Ruins of a thick walled dwelling associated with the Battery on Sion (Hartley's Hill). The walls are at least three feet thick and this was most likely where shot/powder were stored and Artillerymen were stationed. In the background to the right is Sion Hill. Photo by: Co-author Rodger Durham.

Another view of the artillery building ruins on Sion Hill. Photo by: Co-author Rodger Durham.

commonly called Lisis Point." "It is only remarkable for a Military Post during the Insurrection, commanding the Town, one of the principle passes for the Caribs/French into Kingstown, parallel to which it stands within musket shot." *(Note: A smooth bore musket shot is approximately 60-100 yards.)*

Morris – "Du Rumain decided to attack the Fort at Kingstown and as they had begun their advance, they saw about 600 Caribs arriving."

Doctor John Connor testified that when they reached the top of Hartley's Hill (Sion Hill), — "We perceived the Enemy drawing up about a quarter of a mile distant from us." The governor then repeatedly asked what was to be done, saying, "We are a poor Council of War." Addressing himself to the people about him and wishing they would say what was to be done, upon which Colonel Etherington volunteered that he was ready to do anything the governor ordered him.

Morris – "The Governor, and a few others, thought they might manage to keep the Enemy at bay from Zion Hill (Mr. Hartley's Hill) with two pieces of Ordnance until Admirals Byron or Barrington heard of the Attack and came to the rescue; however, both Admirals had gone to Leeward. Even without their help, Morris thought they could hold the Enemy off until Etherington's Troops arrived from his Estate."

Mr. Rellan, when questioned, offered that he thought that the British troops could successfully have held off the enemy, and in fact, he believed they could have driven them from the island. Mr. Campbell concurred, adding that the engineer had said that the ground was strong and that a small number of men might defend it against a much superior force.

Upon Arrival at the top of Mr. Hartley's Hill (Sion Hill)

Doctor John Conner testified, "Having spent a little while on top of Mr. Hartley's Hill considering what might be done, The Governor then proposed, and it was agreed to by all parties, to return to the Fort (Battery) above the Town (Dorchester Hill), where there were two 18 Pounders mounted, and a Proof Magazine adjoining, with an Artillery Store immediately below it. The Governor therefore Ordered the Colonel there with the Troops."

Mr. Fraser no sooner caught up with the group that had taken the main road, having delayed to get arms and ammunition, than he was ordered, along with the rest, to return to the battery above the town (Dorchester Hill).   Soon after reaching there, he saw the enemy on top of Mr. Hartley's Hill (Sion Hill), some of whom were already descending. Doctor Glasgow, in the same situation as Mr. Fraser, said he <u>understood</u> that the troops went to occupy a little fort (battery) behind the town.

Serjeant Major Ayres testified, "When we got up the Hill (Mr. Hartley's Hill, Sion Hill), there was a general cry out for the Troops to go back.   Mr. Richardson added that when the French Troops began their advance, it was first proposed to enter in to the Entrenchments: The Governor and the Colonel step'd aside /as I imagined to confer/ and immediately afterwards a person was dispatched to Order the Troops to return, and go into the Fort (Battery) over the Town (Dorchester Hill), upon which we /the Inhabitants/ all followed them and went into the same Fort (Battery)."

About this same time, Mr. Campbell finally making his way back from viewing the enemy troops at Mr. Crooke's estate, upon his arrival, found that the governor and the troops were headed away, down the hill. He hailed the governor several times and finally was able to get his attention and he turned back to him.

Mr. Campbell reported, "You will be ashamed when you see the *Banditti* you are giving up the Island to; for God's sake, order back the Troops to the Intrenchments, they have time enough still to gain them before the Enemy. To this the Governor responded that Colonel Etherington had march'd back the Troops without any Order from him which he should be answerable for. I then told him, you certainly command Colonel Etherington, and you can Order them back again. He said it was too late, but that he would go with the Troops to the Battery above the Town (Dorchester Hill) which he was determined to defend to the last extremity. I then observed to him that in my opinion, by giving up the Intrenchments and that Hill (Mr. Hartley's Hill, Sion Hill), he had given up the Island, to which he made no answer but went on to the Battery."

The troops are marched back, redirected to the Battery behind the Town (Dorchester Hill), and take up their positions

Serjeant Major Ayres stated that "the Troops went back down the Hill (Mr. Hartley's Hill, Sion Hill) and proceeded to a Hill above the Town (Dorchester Hill). Soon after our arrival there, the Governor,

Colonel Etherington and many other Gentlemen join'd us a little afterwards." In response to questioning, Serjeant McMullan offered that "the Troops had arrived, time enough to have fixed upon the Enemy and that the Governor had Ordered them, and that they were properly Arm'd for defense."

Serjeant Major Ayres, in responding to questioning, stated that there were "about thirty Inhabitants with the Troops, about 10 or 12 Arm'd." As to the nature of the fortification, he answered, "It is a Battery, *en barbette,* with two or three Guns, and was calculated to defend the Bay (Kingstown Bay)."

The Pointing and Attempted Firing of the Gun

Morris – "It was quite clear that Etherington's troops would not reach the entrenchments in time to be of any use and Morris pointed his only Cannon and prepared to fire it. Etherington snatched the lintstock from Morris and restrained him by the arms, preventing him from firing the Gun, shouting all the while, that Ensign Van Hamel was with the French, and to fire upon them would mean the Inhabitants could not expect quarter. Morris later testified that he 'entreated ... the first who should see me turn my back on the Enemy, to lodge the contents of his musket in me,' but this was considered by Etherington to be derogatory to him, 'by assuming an authority he did not think me entitled to.'"

(Note: Again this is from Morris's own later published account as related in Ivor Water's aforementioned biography of him. According to all of the Witnesses, this incident never took place in the manner it was described above, and further, because of the reference to the Entrenchments, it would have taken place on Mr. Hartley's Hill (Sion Hill) and it did not. The issue to fire the Gun or not, took place at the Battery behind the Town.)

Morris – Dr. Thomas Edward Coke, a Methodist missionary and historian, wrote scathingly about Etherington, "...but Colonel Etherington no sooner saw the French were disposed to advance and attack him, than he censured the resolution of the Governor and his Party as the result of inexperience and temerity; he Ordered the Position on Hartley's Hill (Sion Hill) to be evacuated instantaneously, and retreated to the Fort. Then he "ingloriously sued to the Enemy for *Condition,* which his gallantry and conduct might have enabled him to inflict on them a severe punishment, if not a final defeat. Thus did the French avail themselves of the

Defenseless State of the Island, and obtain submission with the trouble of conquest."

(Note: The Witnesses to the first part concerning the giving of Orders for the withdrawal of the Troops from Hartley's Hill (Sion Hill) and the censuring of the resolve of the Governor are not all in agreement. However, this discrepancy is minor to the overall evidences which in fact support Etherington's final claims concerning the sequence of events. It should also be noted that St. Vincent's Historian Charles Shephard, Esq. was extremely critical of Etherington as well with regard to these aspects, although his assertions, like Coke's, are without foundation. Shephard's account is an almost verbatim reprint of the earlier Southey history.)

Doctor Glasgow stated that when he arrived at the battery behind the town (Dorchester Hill), Lieutenant Lees, with the help of several inhabitants, were busy pointing a gun towards the road which it was thought the French must take. "After waiting near three quarters of an hour, the French made their appearance upon Hartley's Hill (Sion Hill) and began to March down the road towards Kingstown." In answer to a question posed by the prosecutor, he said the gun was pointed and proposed to fire about 4:00 o'clock in the afternoon.

Mr. Rellan's version of the *pointing of the Gun and the attempt to fire it*, given in deposition on the 16th June, 1779, /which was the day the French landed in St. Vincent's/ is as follows: "He was in the Fort (the Battery on Dorchester Hill) above the Town of Kingstown. That Governor Morris, Captain Cunningham (Master of a 'Merchant Man') and Mr. Lees, the Engineer, were there, and had pointed an 18 Pounder at the Enemy who were on their March to the Fort. That Governor Morris directed Captain Cunningham, who had a lighted match in his hand, to fire the Gun at the Enemy if they advanced further; that Colonel Etherington thereupon told the Governor that it was more than they durst do, and addressing himself particularly to Mr. Lees, ask'd if he had ever heard of a Gun being fired at the Enemy, after a Flag of Truce had been sent to them and which was not return'd. Mr. Lees answered he knew nothing about it." The deponent, being then ordered away from the fort, did not know what passed there afterwards. Mr. Richardson is in basic agreement with Mr. Rellan's report and he added additionally that he <u>thought</u> that Governor Morris gave orders to fire it — and when prevented by the colonel from doing so, that he did not recollect that the governor further pursued the issue -- and that the colonel did nothing more than that in they way of restraining the firing.

Mr. Campbell concurred with the version.

Doctor John Connor contributed to the description of the event that the Colonel also added that the French troops in sight were only the *advance guard*. Additionally, he testified that when the inhabitants were stopped from firing the first time, they proposed to do it a second time, and were again prevented; at this, Mr. Phipps was sent out to ascertain why the "flag" had been detained and not returned. Shortly thereafter, Mr. Phipps returned and said that the enemy did not consider it as a truce, and would detain it. At this time, an officer and a small party were sent out to cause the enemy to halt their advance; and again the inhabitants wanted to fire the gun this time being prevented from doing so by the governor.

Serjeant Major Ayres testified that soon after arriving at the battery behind the town (Dorchester Hill), "The Enemy appeared on Hartley's Hill (Sion Hill), and an Officer and a Party were Ordered to go /by Governor Morris/ towards the Enemy as an Advanced Guard, but the Officer was very soon call'd back and received some Orders from the Governor, and afterwards went to the Enemy who were then coming down the Hill, and a Corporal, who spoke the French language, was sent after him, both of whom I saw go up to an Officer of the Enemy, who was advanced, and when I saw our Officer rejoin his own Party and the Corporal who was the interpreter came up to the Governor."

Ensign Van Hamel's Detainment

Ensign Van Hamel gave the following evidence: "I was left with the Drummer on the Hill near Mr. Hartley's house, in the charge of a Serjeant and I think 15 or 16 Men, who form'd a circle around me, and the Serjeant received positive Orders not to let me come so near the brow of the Hill as to discover any thing that was going forward in Kingstown. I was afterwards remov'd and kept confined in Mr. Hartley's house, 'till the next morning when I was released by the 'First Article of the Capitulation.'"

Colonel Etherington goes out to the Enemy to discuss Capitulation

Doctor Glasgow gave evidence that the colonel went out to the enemy within three quarters of an hour from the time they arrived at the battery (Dorchester Hill). He said, he and others heard the governor say, "Where can he be going?" After speaking for only a few minutes with the French commandant, he returned and was heard to speak of capitulation, and soon after that, he saw the French commandant making his way to their position. In addition, he heard the colonel say, "It would be the best thing that could ever happen to the Island." And almost at that same instant, a considerable number of Charaibbs appeared on Hartley's Hill (Sion Hill) and that "much alarm'd the Inhabitants, especially those who had Estates thereabouts. They urg'd Capitulation. When the Colonel was ask'd why he thought that Capitulation was best, the Colonel pointed out that when the Island was retaken, the Charaibbs wou'd be driven off the Island, as they had taken an active part. Others of the Inhabitants said it would be a shame to do so." The doctor further added that the governor said he had until 10:00 o'clock the following morning (17th June 1779) to sign the capitulation, by which time he expected Captain Kelly would arrive from the Leeward with the troops. In the meantime, the governor expressed his intention to call a council to deliberate on the terms proposed by the French governor. As to the question, could the governor have called Colonel Etherington back from going out to the enemy, the doctor responded, "...not when I saw him."

Mr. Bolton testified that at about 10:00 o'clock in the morning, he was at the battery (behind the town) and had waited there for some little time when the governor desired the colonel to go out to the enemy. Mr. Bolton testified that it was about 11:30 in the morning when the colonel departed. Doctor Glasgow testified that it was about 4:00 o'clock in the afternoon. Mr. Bolton continued that "the Colonel shortly returned, very alarmed, and *urged a Capitulation,* observing that the French Troops were only an Advanc'd Party." Mr. Fraser added that the governor, "when ask'd whether the Colonel was gone to the Enemy by his Orders, he reply'd, after some hesitation, that he went by his Orders." Mr. Campbell concurred.

Mr. Bolton added to his testimony that nothing particular happened then until about 4:00 o'clock in the afternoon when a "Cessation of Arms" took place and at that time it was announced that the capitulation should be signed at 10:00 o'clock the next morning. Doctor John Conner is in basic agreement with these versions and added that the inhabitants wanted again to fire the gun, and for a fourth time, and they were once again restrained from doing so, this time again by the governor, who voiced concern that they might hit the colonel. Doctor Glasgow agreed that it was the governor who stopped them from firing. When asked in what manner the colonel *urged a capitulation,* Mr. Bolton replied that it lay in the proposal 'that the French Troops were only an Advanced

Party' and 'supposing that the French Troops were so much superior'. When asked, Mr. Bolton stated that only two or three of the inhabitants were in favour of capitulation.

Doctor John Connor said of the incident, "The Colonel soon (after being sent out) return'd, and after a conversation with the Governor, the Governor delar'd that a Capitulation had been ask'd for, and that he was offered the same as was granted at Dominique. The Governor then ask'd the Inhabitants if such a Capitulation wou'd be agreeable to them. All except two answered that it would not, and they said the Island was going to be given away Treacherously, and Infamously, and desired the Governor to recollect, that the Island was not taken, but *given away.*" Serjeant Major Ayres agreed with this version and added only that afterwards of making the announcement, the governor mounted his horse and went to town, followed by the inhabitants, and that the troops remained in the battery (at Dorchester Hill) 'till the colours were struck the next day.

Mr. Rellan gave evidence that the Colonel, upon his return from the meeting with the French, *appeared to be in great confusion* and *not anxious to engage the Enemy.* When asked to elaborate he said, "...he told Governor Morris that the Articles of Capitulation were agreed upon, and the Fort and Out Posts should be given up by 4:00 o'clock in the afternoon (of the 16th); upon which Governor Morris took out his watch and said that it was then half past two 'clock and therefore quite impossible. The Colonel answered that the Fort must be delivered up at that time. The Governor declared that he would not give it up until the Capitulation was signed. Upon which the Colonel said that if it was not, the Enemy wou'd March in and *cut their throats;* thereupon, many of the Principle Gentlemen of the Island struck their Firelocks against the Ground, being much vexed at the Colonel's expression." Doctor John Connor added to Mr. Rellan's report, "The Governor then desir'd the Colonel to return to the Officer Commanding the French Troops, requesting until the next morning to sign the Capitulation. The Colonel accordingly went and brought back word that it was agreed to. Upon which, the Governor desired the Inhabitants to return to their respective habitations, and said that a Capitulation was agreed upon, and that there was not further use for their staying where they were. At this time, many other Inhabitants, who had gone home to fetch their Arms, were on their March to join us, but on hearing that a Capitulation was agreed upon, they dispersed and went back to their houses. The Troops still kept possession of the Fort (Battery)."

Serjeant Major Ayres, "…soon after I heard the Governor call the Gentlemen of the Island into a small house in the Battery (Dorchester Hill) I approach'd the window, and heard him ask their opinion what he should do. They, in general, spoke against defending the Island and wanted a Capitulation, which I thought from their conversation was agreed upon. As soon as the Governor came out of the house he call'd to the Colonel and sent him off to the Enemy."

Serjeant Major Ayres, under questioning, agreed that the colonel was sent out to the enemy, a second time, by the governor. Some of the inhabitants who had not been in the house (the meeting that took place after the first return of the colonel) asked the governor what he had resolved upon and what he would do. The governor said he had "Ordered the Colonel to obtain for them the 'Capitulation of Dominique' and said he was to ask two or three more Articles, which if the Enemy wou'd not grant, he was to take the 'Dominique Capitulation'; the Colonel went to the Enemy and talked a while with them."

Serjeant Major Ayres was asked by Colonel Etherington if he was present when the governor ordered him the first and second time to the enemy and he responded that he was. When asked what the Governor said upon his return from the second time he testified that the Governor said "he was happy to have got the Capitulation of Dominica, and he told the Inhabitants that they might return to their houses." Serjeant McMullan was in total agreement. Mr. Rellan also said that he thought the colonel was sent out twice.

Mr. Campbell testified, with regard to the capitulation, that he heard the colonel speak of it and took him to be the proposer and added that he also heard him speak of the French troops, in view, as being only an advance of the enemy and there was a greater force in the rear. At just that moment, Mr. Campbell received a letter from the Windward part of the island mentioning that three ships, under English colours, were in view. He offered that they might be the enemy and suggested that this might be the basis upon which Etherington proposed what they saw before them was only an advanced guard.

Morris – Again, according to his own account (via Water's): "Morris thought Etherington's behaviour bordered on criminality but he didn't see that he had any choice but to surrender. The Governor sent Mr. Phipps to receive the French Proposals and Etherington rode after him without the Governor's authority. The Proposals they brought back were for an unconditional surrender which Morris rejected out-of-hand, and he and Mons. De Canonge negotiated for the balance of the afternoon, Morris playing for time in hopes that the Navy would arrive to save them. About 4:30 in the afternoon, the Preliminary Articles were agreed to and the two French Officers (De Canonge and Du Rumain) were discussing the Capitulation when Du Rumain saw two English ships, in full sail, entering the Bay (Kingstown Bay). The discussion was promptly put aside and the French rushed off to affect a capture."

(Note: Morris's account with regard to Etherington riding without his authority is not supported by the Evidences.)

Mr. Bolton stated that "about 3:00 or 4:00 o'clock in the afternoon, the French Commandant came to the Court House in the Town of Kingstown, where was a Lawyer named Burke, who he believed was to draw out the Terms of Capitulation," and added that he saw the colonel and the governor go there about an hour afterwards. Mr. Bolton then went home. The Colonel asked him if he saw him go into the Court House and he answered that he didn't remember, but that he did see them together some time afterwards.

Dr. Glasgow, upon questioning, was asked "if he saw the French Commandant in the Fort on that evening (16th June 1779) and he replied that he did see him very near it." He went on to relate that he had overheard the Governor say that "they were preparing a Capitulation but that he did not hear the Colonel speak any thing" and then admitted that he didn't recall the colonel being present. When asked of the whereabouts of the King's troops, he said that they remained at the fort (the battery on Dorchester Hill).

The Capitulation

(Note: The actual state of the island's defenses at this time was frightful. A multitude of factors contributed to this deplorable state; British troops were widely scattered and unable to join up at Kingstown in time to defend it as a united force (aside from insufficient numbers), a poorly trained (essentially non-existent) militia, depleted provision and ammunition stores, no available Royal Naval support, and low morale. As such, there is no question but that a show of "resistance" would have had disastrous results.)

Morris – "According to his own account, Morris tried to conceal the weakness of his position, still hoping that help would come from the

Navy. He continued to parley all night, until forced by *fear of the savage Black Caribs*, that they might be turned loose. He agreed to surrender on Terms."

According to Doctor John Connor, the governor had received permission from the Council to sign the Capitulation the next morning, the troops still in possession of the fort (the battery on Dorchester Hill), and he had witnessed that the French frigates who had earlier chased a vessel in the morning (16th June 1779), had fallen to Leeward and could not fetch back into the bay (Kingstown Bay). The governor, seeing this, "seem'd sorry for what had happen'd and he and the Colonel condem'd each other for it. The Governor declar'd that he did not think himself bound to adhere to this Agreement and would assemble all the Force he could by the next morning, and find some means to break through it." In consequence of this, several of the inhabitants assembled again. Mr. Campbell and the doctor inquired of the colonel "if the Troops were coming down from Leeward and if any thing was to be done. The Colonel answered that if the Troops were Ordered Up he wou'd engage and that they wou'd arrive by nine the next morning."

Doctor Patrick Connor, under questioning, stated that when he first heard that the Capitulation was agreed upon was on the evening of the 16th June 1779.

Doctor Glasgow stated that he <u>believed</u> the Capitulation was signed the next day (17th June 1779); in addition he volunteered that Captain Kelly and his troops didn't arrive until the 17th.

Doctor John Connor continued his testimony, "...that upon hearing there was a Council the next morning (17th June 1779) at Government House, I went there and I heard the Governor, at that time, say to the Colonel the following words, —'Did I not tell you Colonel, two or three days ago, that I had certain information that this Island was to be attacked?' The Colonel said to this, 'yes you did, but you have had so many reports of the same thing, that I did not believe it; and that if the Governor knew of it, why did he not prepare for it.'" In response to a question, had the French commandant suppered with the governor on the night of the 16th, the doctor answered he didn't know but that he saw him at the governor's and when asked if he had suppered there he said, "I have <u>forgot</u>;" and when asked if the colonel had, he said, "I do not recollect."

Ensign Van Hamel testified that on this morning, when he came to Kingstown, he went to the court house where he saw the governor, with Capitulation in hand, addressing himself to some of his Council, a Mr. Hewit, the Receiver General, and several other of the town's people, in these words, viz. "Gentlemen, I have done all in my power to get you the Capitulation of Dominica which I am happy I have obtained." They all congratulated him upon the occasion, and "say'd they were much oblig'd to him."

Doctor George Young, the only witness for the Defense, and at this time a Council Member, was ask'd by the colonel if he (the colonel) was present when the Council Members were preparing the Capitulation and the doctor answered that he was not.

Morris – "When Du Rumain returned (from the expedition against the English Ships that has come into the Bay) and reviewed the Articles, he would not agree to them even though signed by Mons. De Canonge, stating that they were contrary to his Orders from Admiral D'Estaing. In particular, he demanded that the Treaty with the Black Caribs be examined and that England be made to compensate them for 'bad treatment.' He threatened to tear up the Agreement and said he would look on the Island as taken by *Unconditional Conquest*."

Morris – At this point in the treaty negotiations, Chatoyer (the Black Carib war-chief), had been "asked by Du Rumain about land encroachments perpetrated on them by the British," to which the chief specifically mentioned Etherington's land. Governor Morris, however, persuaded the French commandant that this should be addressed in a civil court, and, therefore, being inappropriate to include in the treaty.

(Note: This aspect will be further discussed in the Epilogue section.)

Morris – "Morris continued to insist on the Terms of the Treaty he had signed with Mons. De Canonge, and finally Du Rumain agreed; they had copies made in English and French and the Parties signed."

Doctor Glasgow, upon questioning, stated that the governor had signed the Capitulation.

Mr. Rellan stated that the possession of the fort by the French occurred after the signing of the treaty.

Morris – According to his sequence of events, on the 18th June 1779, the Surrender of St. Vincent's was completed.

Regarding the treaty itself, more in-depth commentary will be made on the specific terms in the Epilogue section during final

One of the original 39 cannons that were at later built Fort Charlotte and currently on display at the fort. Photo by: Co-author Rodger Durham.

summary comments. However, it should be noted here that **Mr. Rellan's** testimony added, "The Deponent further says that about three days after the Island was Surrendered to the French, he heard *very high words* pass between the Colonel and Governor Morris respecting the signing of some papers, the contents of which he is ignorant of, but was later *informed* by Governor Morris's Clerk, that these papers were concerning the Distribution of Troops at St. Vincent's, prior to the Landing of the Enemy."

(Note: Thus, in essence there is no direct evidence whatsoever from other witnesses as to any argument between Etherington and Morris regarding the auspices of specific terms other than the colonel's and governor's own statements.)

Later, **Sir William Young (son)** commented on aspects which basically point to the vulnerability aspects of the island including the full support and loyalty of the Caribs to the French, which supports Etherington's own defense claims - "Count D'Estaing, Commander-in-Chief, to shew the high sense he entertained for the Black Charaib's services in the Enterprize, appointed their Friend and Leader, Perchin La Roche, to be the Lieutenant-Governor of St. Vincent's: The Charaibs returned the compliment with "active service."[115]

On the other hand, later island historian **Doctor Alexander Anderson** (second curator of the Botanic Gardens) comments about the physical aspects of the island which would perhaps lend some support (although not entirely) to Morris's position of having the advantage and thereby his reasoning for holding out to the end - "The French conquered the Island and selected for their Garrison, Dorchester Hill (the Hill behind the Town). The point of the strategic importance of Dorchester Hill is well taken." He further commented, "...in later years, Dorchester Hill was resigned for a Hill on the West side of the Bay (Berkshire Hill, location of the barracks, i.e. the later site of Fort Charlotte as previously mentioned), of small extent, consequently easier defended."[116]

⊕ EPILOGUE

At this point, some final extensive comment summarizing the entire affair is necessary to place "the controversy" in more proper perspective. At first glance, it would appear that Etherington was perhaps most responsible for the loss of St. Vincent's. However, a more thorough evaluation and review of the succession of events as has been discussed does not support this or the allegations, and reveals why the Lieutenant Colonel was appropriately acquitted of the same.

First, one later historian openly critical of Etherington suggests that it is essentially "immaterial" in reviewing the contents of the Dominica-like surrender terms agreed to at St. Vincent's.[117] This assertion could not be more incorrect since those terms were most favorable to the inhabitants of the island including allowing them to "go freely to their homes..." and stipulating that "the governor, staff officers (and their wives), soldiers and artillerymen, to be carried to the island of Antigua...at the expense of His Most Christian Majesty [the French King], and there to be at liberty to do duty...[and] be exchanged for an equal number of French prisoners."[118] The inhabitants were also allowed to continue their civil government and commerce as previous under the protection of the French King, retain their possessions (although not their arms), and enjoy free exercise of their religion among other concessions. Had Etherington not accepted terms at all (as Morris claims, although both claimed each other as responsible for the terms as was noted in the testimony), it is very probable that the inhabitants would have suffered further personal violence and pillage at the hands of the French and Caribs, which is, in fact, exactly what happened some two weeks later when the British Governor there refused terms during the subsequent French invasion of nearby Grenada.[119] This is further supported by Governor Morris's own admission that he signed the terms for "fear that the savage Caribs would be let loose".[120] Moreover, even more damaging to Morris's case was that this did indeed happen as proved by the destruction and pillaging that occurred when the Caribs swept down the coast at St. Vincent's after landing with the French as previously described. It is also interesting to note the response of the planters and other British inhabitants of the island. From the testimony in the trial, it is evident that most of the "militia" were initially opposed to the surrender of the island without a fight. However, the zeal for this potential endeavor was quickly abandoned when they were confronted with the aspects of a Carib reign of terror, a wise decision since these civilians were so ill equipped, poorly trained, and simply would have been no match for the force to be engaged, irrespective of either the French or the Caribs.

While it is obvious that no commanding officer would ever desire having to consider terms of capitulation, certainly Etherington cannot be faulted for encouraging the acceptance of such generous terms under the circumstances, even if he only supported those as he claimed, as opposed to having been the actual author of the same. Facing such an overwhelming force in numbers (the official French count of the British troops eventually exchanged at Antigua was 287, not all of which were regular infantry as this also included plantation owners and other colonists[121]), with poorly constructed and undermanned defenses, raw recruits (described as totally unfit) and no assembled formal militia support, it seems the better part of valor that Etherington chose such an honorable surrender that would avoid unnecessary further casualties and essentially ensure that his troops would be available to fight the enemy at some future date. This is not a far-fetched or unreasonable idea. On the contrary, it was, in fact, an acceptable option for military commanders in the mid-eighteenth century as advocated by Sebastien le Prestre de Vauban (1633-1707), a French military engineer. Vauban was considered the most renowned authority on siege and warfare tactics by that time, and his treatises were widely used by both the French and British military.[122] The same can be said for the assertions of temerity. Should the mere act of surrendering have been held as grounds for conviction as pure dereliction of duty, let alone cowardice and/or treason that Morris also accused Etherington of, then even General Lord Charles Cornwallis would surely have been found guilty as such for his surrender at Yorktown in 1781 to end the war, and not rewarded in future years as the Commander-in-Chief and Viceroy of India and Ireland.

An equally important point that should not be overlooked in relation to the preceding aspects is the fact that Etherington was adamant about not opening fire on the French during the "flag of truce" or parley, in particular since Ensign Van Hamel was still being held by them after being illegally detained in violation of the well-accepted general "rules of war." To do so otherwise, as Morris had wanted, would have been a breach of honor and trust, although certainly an argument could be made that it was already obvious the French had no intention of conducting their offensive by accepted war etiquette. Although perhaps a minor consideration in the overall picture of this controversy, Etherington deserves commendation for standing his ground in this instance, which is hardly grounds for "conduct unbecoming an officer."

An incidental and tangential aspect that is deserving of at least brief mention at this point is the fact that historically, St. Vincent's Island is noted for having been "surrendered without firing a shot." While this in essence is true with regard to the actual time of the surrender negotiations, it is technically incorrect since there the gallant stand was made at the Colonarie post as previously noted.

Secondly, the allegations and/or suggestions of treason and monetary bribery (the latter being suggested by one later historian[123]) are frivolous as no credible witness or evidence was ever produced. The undeniable reality of the human condition is such that temptation may present itself to anyone, however, it is highly unlikely, given Etherington's known and previously demonstrated reputation as a "very good and loyal officer," that he engaged in accepting any such alleged considerations. Had even the smallest amount of evidence to substantiate these charges existed, Etherington would certainly have been cashiered from the King's service and thus would not have received promotion to full colonel in the army three years later as eventually occurred.

Third, as to the charge that Etherington disobeyed the governor's orders concerning the actual military defense plan for the island, this is most debatable. Believing an eventual French (and Carib) invasion to be highly possible, Governor Morris had directed in 1778 that "all the posts be manned...and if the Caribs remained neutral when the island was invaded, the troops were to follow the enemy down the Windward coast...(to reinforce the governor at Kingstown)...but if the Caribs attacked, the troops were to counter-attack, and hide their wives and children to draw the Caribs back."[124] As has been described, it is obvious that Etherington did not follow this exact plan, again having the majority of Royal American troops stationed on his estate. However, it is of vital importance to scrutinize several factors specifically related to this in considering the charges of dereliction of duty and having troops employed for personal purposes.

One of the primary and most critical charges (even perhaps the most damaging charge among all those filed) that Morris as well as later historians all leveled against Etherington was the alleged use of troops for clearing of land on his estate. As now seen from the actual trial transcripts, this is erroneous as there was no proof or credible evidence whatsoever to substantiate this from anyone including soldiers under Etherington's own command at the site. This is even more absurd since it was revealed in sworn testimony that the troops were performing those activities for the purpose of constructing a post with barracks "on Etherington's land" which was ordered built by Morris himself. That the governor would even chance filing such charges borders on hypocrisy.

Furthermore, the remaining posts were garrisoned with small detachments of Royal American troops dispersed as best as possible, and Etherington did reconnoiter and eventually reinforce the Governor. In addition, it is not unreasonable (or inappropriate) to consider what might have transpired had the gunner at the Hyde's Point Battery been allowed to fire on the approaching vessels, thus deterring or at least delaying the French advance plundering the countryside and providing more time for the reinforcement troops from the 60th to come to aid.

Nonetheless, whether one specific plan was followed or not, the situation that resulted was a consequence of an important consideration that cannot be overlooked. It is well known that disagreement existed between British military and governmental officials during the 18th century as to who had rightful authority for military decisions throughout the various colonies. Certainly both Morris and Etherington believed themselves as having that authority alone, and it is apparent from their actions that each acted accordingly, although Etherington saw this in a somewhat different and more specific degree. It is clear from the testimony from all parties, including Etherington, that the governor had the final say in the military decisions for the island's defense while Etherington had the actual command of the troops *to implement any particular actions as directed by* the governor. Morris himself, "as Commander-in-Chief (of the civil government and militia)...took this instruction to mean what it said" in the defense plans for the island,[125] although, again as later noted this was considered by Etherington as "...assuming an authority he did not think me [Morris] entitled to."

In many instances, however, the British government viewed the actual military commanding officer as the definitive authority in such matters.[126] This was particularly true in the Caribbean as regular military troops were responsible to the civil colonial governors in peacetime.[127] Yet, this dichotomy was, without question, one of the major problems responsible for the fate of the island. Although King George later expressed disappointment that Etherington had not offered some specific personal thoughts as to defense measures, the officer would probably not have been acquitted on that account, not to mention the debacle that would have occurred had he accepted total command and actually initiated such military action. It is clear from the testimony, however, that Morris was not about to give up his command authority to Etherington in any circumstance, despite the governor's lack of experience and knowledge in military matters.

There is yet another serious aspect, which is, in essence, the underlying factor provoking this entire matter, and that is the personality conflict that existed between Morris and Etherington. Aside from the above noted dispute over military authority, there is no doubt that the personal feud over the St. Vincent's land grant controversy between the two contributed to their further animosity and distrust toward each other. The governor had been opposed to the sale of Carib lands on St. Vincent's to individuals, and particularly to Etherington as previously discussed. Believing that the Caribs would still claim some rights to the land despite their having sold or granted away parcels to colonists, Morris had his own ideas as to how the land should be obtained and eventually settled for future crop plantations and other development on the island. As such, he assumed the authority to make land grants in smaller parcels to individuals and/or quick-rents, acquiring the land "from the Caribs in the King's Name," and thus avoiding any potential Carib claims.

There were problems with this plan, however, in that large valuable land grants had already been made to absentees by the British government, including one 4000 acre tract to General Robert Monckton (who had commanded the British expedition against the French at Martinique in 1762; and aside from Etherington's land grant promised by the Caribs as previously mentioned). Further still, resulting from his continuous disputes with the inhabitants of St. Vincent's, there were complaints by the Assembly that the governor was making grants in an unfair manner and had reserved larger grants for himself and his sister (his own three being 500, 350, and 360 acres respectively). Morris would counter that he was falsely accused and that the list of grants was a forgery, which in actuality was true to some degree. He was, however, admonished by Lord Germain and even King George himself for "granting away His Majesty's lands in the island of St. Vincent's in the most wanton manner, without any advice of your Council...and it is His Majesty's pleasure that...you [Morris] do immediately desist from practices so disadvantageous, prejudicial, and detrimental to the public, upon pain of His Majesty's highest displeasure."[128]

As far as the Etherington grant, it will be recalled that Morris later accused him of illegally" persuading" the Assembly of approving the sale of the land from Chief Chatoyer and his fellow Caribs "while the Governor was on leave from the island" for a time in 1776-77. This is somewhat puzzling since; again, it is known that Etherington had been given the land grant from the Caribs three years prior in 1773. Until recently, however, it was unclear whether or not by 1776 Etherington had perhaps made an agreement to actually compensate the Caribs for their land. The latter would seem less likely, as even Morris himself stated that the Caribs "...will forego anything for such [vanity and attachment to glaring, uncommon, conspicuous ornaments] when for money, or even terrors, they will do nothing."[129] On the other hand, it is known that the Caribs did accept money in exchange for lands, including Chatoyer who eventually became very wealthy himself as prior discussed. This, in fact, is exactly what happened as evidenced by Etherington's recently located "Memorial to the Treasury Board," in which he confirms that not only did Chatoyer and his fellow chiefs (including his own brothers) agree to the purchase and had actually accepted initial payments knowing the land was within the Carib treaty boundary, but they also did so as a means of expressing gratitude "chiefly in acknowledgement of certain services your said Memorialist has for these past two years done to the whole body of the Charibs...more...than in consideration of any money which they have received already or expect to receive from him hereafter."[130]

Furthermore, Chief Chatoyer would actually recant his story later during negotiations of terms for the surrender of the island. When asked by the French commandant M. Du Rumain if he had any grievances, the chief alleged "he and his brothers and other chiefs had been deceived, both as to quantity and terms, respecting land bought from them by Etherington."[131] Chatoyer's claim is suspect, yet not surprising for several obvious reasons. Chatoyer and the other Caribs had never accepted the British nor the terms of the 1773 treaty, and despite pretending to profess friendship and a willingness to live peacefully sharing St. Vincent's, they did in fact join the French cause (whom they did not entirely trust either) to eliminate the British and regain their island. The Caribs in this respect were no different from many of the North American Indian tribes during the 18th century who had (understandably) no loyalty to their "professed" allies and would often change allegiance even in the midst of a battle to whichever side appeared emerging as the victor. It is further suspect in that not only had Etherington's land been offered in 1773, long before the land controversy re-emerged, but Chatoyer would have known it was within the treaty boundary as well and as evidenced by the 1776 Byres map as noted. Had he really objected to Etherington acquiring the tract for the latter reason alone, (regardless of the acreage amount and whether or not it was to be an outright grant or the later agreed purchase), Chatoyer certainly would not have consented to the same. Nor is it likely that Lord Germain would have appointed Etherington as military commandant at St. Vincent's for the reasons he stated, had the Lieutenant Colonel not been on good terms with the natives. The latter is most inconsistent with Etherington's known and precedent reputation, and further raises (not unreasonably) some questions as to Chatoyer's credibility concerning the matter. Unfortunately, no additional information has been located to date, which might clarify this portion of the controversy.

Some comment is appropriate concerning the court-martial itself. That the officers of the preliminary court of inquiry would order Etherington to stand trial is not surprising given General Gage's, known propensity to make judgments based on only one side of a dispute and before having all relevant facts,[132] as well as General Tryon's previous conflicts with colonists during his tenures as colonial governor of North Carolina and later New York in the American colonies prior to the Revolution. As for supporters of Governor Morris, who would claim the outcome a result of the trial being "done in so negligent and discreditable a manner, that the whole business became a mockery,"[133] this is an understandable (albeit expected) reaction given the governor's extreme dislike of Etherington. Nor was any evidence in support of such a charge borne out in testimony during the trial, and if it did exist, the witnesses for the prosecution have no one to blame but themselves for not speaking out to expose any relevant facts regarding the same.

Furthermore, the court-martial was "most unusual" with respect to the way it was conducted. The prosecution witness list was made up of nearly as many Morris supporters/Etherington detractors as Etherington supporters, four of the thirteen actually being in his command. The prosecutor, during the examination of the witnesses, often as not, let them *ramble on* even though it was obvious that the testimony they were giving was contrary to the Prosecutor's case; often, even the Prosecutor's line of questioning seemed to follow this style as well. The President of the Court, much astonished that the Defense only had one witness, asked the Deputy Judge Advocate, "Were the Officers of the 60th Regiment inform'd that a general Court-martial was to be held on the Prisoner, and that all Evidences were to Attend?" The reply was, "Yes, the Commander-in-Chief announced this trial in Public Orders, dated at Head Quarters the 30th September 1781." Captain Kelly was the only officer from the 60th in attendance and his testimony supported Etherington's position entirely. The other aspect that can legitimately be considered as detrimental to the prosecution was the absence of Morris himself, through no fault of his own, having been detained in Antigua by one of his creditors as prior noted.

Finally, in all fairness, Lieutenant Colonel Etherington without a doubt must share some responsibility for his conduct with regard to the affair. He perhaps could have formulated a more specific and precautionary defense plan, as suggested by His Majesty King George III in his full approval of the verdict, although it is highly unlikely the "raw recruits" comprising the bulk of the 60th troops would have been an effective fighting unit due to the limited time they had been in service. Notwithstanding, it is quite obvious that Governor Morris was attempting to "find a scapegoat" for the loss of St. Vincent's (since he had the ultimate responsibility for the island's defense), and thus, in effect, downplay his own involvement in the multitude of contributing factors to the end result, not the least of which entailed the lack of an organized militia that further weakened the island's defense capacity. This is, in fact, most evident in subsequent letters by the governor to Lord William Shelburne, successor to Germain, including one sent fully two years after the trial verdict had been rendered, wherein Morris actually admits that capitulation was the better option against overwhelming odds and in essence (and ironically although not intentionally) supports Etherington's own defense.[134]

Clearly, though, both Morris and Etherington must share responsibility for the eventual capitulation. To lay blame solely to either is simply unfair and would invite indignation. However, as is evident by the trial testimony, it is also clear as to why Etherington was appropriately acquitted of all charges with the court declaring them as "groundless and malicious." As previously noted, this is yet another example of the conflict and, in essence, folly between military and civilian officials concerning military authority that was ever so common and which plagued the British government throughout the 18th century. Summarily, the *root* of the problem, as the historical record has shown, was the inability and unwillingness of the British government to lend sufficient support to the island when it was needed i.e. lack of efficient Naval support in the Caribbean, few troops, widely scattered, insufficient and poorly garrisoned posts). The upshot of the whole situation was that both Morris and Etherington were eventually exonerated, and the government "got off scot-free," without having to endure the slightest criticism, at least in the case of St. Vincent's.

THE FATE OF...

Following the capture of St. Vincent's, activities in the Caribbean theatre of the American Revolution continued. The military and civil events involving the West Indies during this period have been well documented, and while not the focus of this present work, it will suffice to say that they have been considered a vital factor in the eventual victory for independence by the American colonies.[135] At St. Vincent's, the year following its surrender, a devastating hurricane hit the island with all buildings being destroyed[136] and a later smallpox epidemic occurred, resulting in the deaths of many Black Caribs. The population at this time had seen an increase in Black slaves to work on the sugar plantations as most of the British settlers, although much harassed by the Black Caribs, would remain during the entire French occupation in the ensuing years.

In December of 1780, British armament appeared off Calliaqua in St. Vincent's, under the command of Admiral George Rodney and General Sir John Vaughan in an attempt to retake the island. However, the British troops that landed withdrew after one day as a result of heavy resistance by the Black Caribs (assisting some of the French settlers) who killed both black and white inhabitants during the destruction of numerous plantations.[137]

By 1781, the tide had turned in North America. During the time of Etherington's trial, General George Washington and Comte De Rochambeau had trapped the British Army at Yorktown in Virginia. The French fleet under De Grasse had blockaded the Chesapeake Bay cutting off any escape route, and eventually on 17 October 1781, the infamous British surrender was completed, essentially ending the war in the American colonies. The French naval forces under De Grasse then proceeded to the Caribbean corridor, and with assistance of the Spanish, had planned a "Grand Attack" on Jamaica. Britain had cause for concern as the French in a series of successes in the Caribbean had taken Dominica, St. Vincent's, Grenada, Tobago, Demerara, Essequibo, Berbice by this time, and then subsequently, St. Kitts, Montserrat, and Nevis in 1782.[138]

However, the French were defeated by the British fleet, under Admiral George Rodney the following year in a massive naval encounter known as the "Battle of the Saints" between Martinique and Guadeloupe, thereby securing British naval dominance in the Caribbean, and earning Rodney eventual elevation to the title of Lord Rodney.

During the four years of French occupancy, the French paid little attention to the Island of St. Vincent's and it continued to operate they way it had prior to the surrender, including the government. After a series of five French governors, on 28 January 1783, the British eventually regained St. Vincent's and several others of its West Indies islands as a result of the Peace Treaty of Versailles. Edmund Lincoln, Esq., on the 3rd March, was appointed Captain-General and Governor-in-Chief of the Island of St. Vincent's.[139] On 30 November, the Provisional Articles of Peace were signed between England and the United States, granting the latter's independence, and thereby officially ending the American Revolutionary War in the Caribbean corridor as well.

As for the Island of St. Vincent's, what became of the principle adversaries and participants who were so entangled in the events cumulating in the ignominious surrender in 1779 is most intriguing. **Lieutenant Colonel Etherington's** military career was to continue in a favorable realm. He remained in the Caribbean for some time after his acquittal. In 1782, he was transferred back to the First Battalion, receiving promotion to colonel in the army on 16 May according to the British Army Lists.[140] Apparently he made no effort to recover his estate in St. Vincent's as later it was, at least partially, made into a "reservation" for the few Caribs who escaped exportation to Roatan at the end of the Second Carib/French War in 1795. Etherington simply abandoned the estate when he departed the West Indies with the regiment in 1787, and whether he ever returned to visit is unknown. His land today remains undeveloped and the extreme high, forested terrain presents a beautiful scene. Etherington is further noted as commanding officer of the First Battalion 60th in Jamaica and then Halifax, Nova Scotia both in 1787.[141] By this time, both remaining 60th Battalions were stationed in North America, the First at Halifax and the Second at Montreal.[142]

It had been previously assumed he died in England in 1787 or 1788 after accompanying the regiment there when it was recalled at the end of the Revolution.[143] However, a recent important discovery has revealed the date of his *retirement* from the British Army as 15 January 1788,[144] although the date of his death remains as yet unknown. His original portrait which was previously unknown to

Signature of George Etherington.
Photocopy of his original signature, Courtesy: Public Record Office,
Kew, Surrey, England (PRO/WO, 34/49, ff. 162-63.

exist was recently discovered and is currently on display at the Royal Green Jackets Museum (formerly the King's Royal Rifle Corps, i.e. the 60th Royal American Regiment) in Winchester, England. Having been donated to the museum in 1994, a meticulous evaluation process by Major General Giles Mills, the 60th Historian, Museum staff, and portrait experts from Christies, the famed Brokerage/Antique Appraisal and Auction Firm, has concluded that all evidence to date suggests this splendid portrait is almost certainly that of Lieutenant Colonel Etherington. It has been attributed to John Trotter, an 18th Century portrait artist who was based in Dublin, Ireland, and it could have been painted when Etherington disembarked there on return from Halifax with the regiment in 1787.[145]

A description of the portrait at the museum states that it "shows Lt. Col. Etherington to be seated overlooking the land granted him by the warlike Carib Indians in North Eastern St. Vincent's in the Caribbean in 1773; the bivouac of his Light Company is in the forest behind." It also depicts an older, distinguished looking officer, and "Etherington was then at least 50 years of age. He is seen wearing the 60th uniform, laid down in the Warrant of 1768, except that he is wearing short gaiters and no black stock or sword belt, concessions to the heat of the Caribbean." In all, aside from being an important recent find regarding Etherington himself, it is also a beautiful example of surviving 18th-century portrait art.

Finally, in assessing Etherington's career, it is evident that he was well liked by his men, and a loyal, dedicated officer of the King who went about accomplishing his duties and responsibilities in a quiet demeanor. Although not a remarkable officer, he was, nonetheless, a most capable one, and despite the enigma concerning his actions at Michilimackinac in 1763 and St. Vincent's in 1779, he retained a good reputation among his superior officers and proceeded on to complete a well-respected career in the British Army.

Valentine Morris, Esq., Etherington's adversary, after being also exonerated of all charges concerning the surrender of St. Vincent's, was not as fortunate. His overdrafts of funds for the island while in office as governor at St. Vincent's were seen as overzealous spending and eventually remanded to King's Bench Debtor's Prison as the British government persisted in refusing to reimburse him for his personal expenses on behalf of the island. His creditors, aware that he still had properties, kept him in prison for five years before he yielded and sold them, including his beloved Piercefield estate in

Wales.[146] Upon his release, his wife having earlier been confined to a "mad house," he went to live with his sister. On 26 August 1789, Valentine Morris died in London, at her house, "a poor and broken man," sadly, all his good intentions being essentially overshadowed by his propensity for wealth, power, and perhaps a touch of arrogance. His Piercefield house today near Chepstow in south Wales is a preserved roofless shell, although local organizations and societies hope to have the ruins of the mansion restored to its previous grand elegance someday.[147]

Perhaps the most unfortunate of the three principle participants relating to the Etherington court-martial and this St. Vincent's saga is **Chatoyer**, the Black Caribs' War-Chief. Having remained on the island as their leader, as previously mentioned, he and his brother DuVallee became quite wealthy. However, he and the Caribs continued their resistance to the British in defending what remained of their homeland against further land encroachment by greedy plantation owners and settlers. Despite this, he did remain friends with Sir William Young, who in 1792 gave him a silver mounted sword that had belonged to Young's brother Henry Young, who had "died with the same in his hand at Saratoga" during the American Revolution in New York back in 1777, while Prince William Henry had also given him a silver gorget.[148] Chatoyer and his Caribs joined forces once again with the French in a last attempt to drive the British from St. Vincent's at the outset of the Second Carib/French War in 1796. He was killed in March that year during a battle by Major Alexander Leith of the island's militia "in a hand-to-hand fight, bayoneted in a cane field"[149] on Dorchester Hill, near Hartley's Hill overlooking Kingstown where Etherington and Morris had quarreled seventeen years before. The location of his grave is unknown, although a monument to him was established on Dorchester Hill and still remains today. What became of his silver sword and gorget remains a mystery as well. At the conclusion of the war, the British having succeeded in defeating them, most of the Black Caribs were removed from the island and shipped off to Roatan. Chatoyer is recognized as a hero in St. Vincent's history and a few people of Black Carib descent still reside on the island.[150]

The further history of St. Vincent's, including this Second Carib War, the abolishment of slavery and development of the plantations into the 20th century is as fascinating as these earlier events, although is beyond the intent of this book. In brief summary, however, the island eventually became a part of the British Colony of the

Windward Islands in 1871. Much later in 1969, it was afforded status as a British Associated State before full independence in the British Commonweath was designated in 1979 and the country being officially known as **St. Vincent's and the Grenadines**. Today, these islands continue to comprise a picturesque panorama of beauty as part of the Windward Islands in the Eastern Caribbean (Lesser Antilles) and a popular destination for tourists and cruise ships from all over the world. Agriculture has remained as St. Vincent's principal industry producing arrowroot, bananas, cotton and other crops.

Spectacular views from St. Vincent's mountains and coastline abound with beautiful trees, flowers and beaches remaining essentially as they did back in the 1770's. Kingstown, the busy capital retains much of its historic flavor as it did during the colonial times as well and has a variety of restaurants providing fine dining, boutiques and art galleries, as well as fun shopping in the historic downtown waterfront, and numerous resorts for vacation enjoyment. While some historic buildings remain, others unfortunately lie in ruins (such as Mr. Hartley's House and the battery on Sion Hill) although sites of many of the batteries and fortifications that were present during Etherington's and Morris's times can be seen today. Some archaeological investigations have taken place in recent years despite slow progress due to lack of funding and much remains to be done, hopefully in future years. A few previously mentioned sites have been preserved and are worth spending the time to visit. Among these are the preserved famous Botanic Gardens (the oldest such gardens in the Western Hemisphere) and Fort Charlotte built in 1806 (on the site of the earlier Barracks where Etherington assembled the 60th in 1779 before the capitulation and standoff with Morris) and which houses a colorful museum of Black Carib history.

Finally, for those interested persons having the ambition and time, a drive to the more wilderness northern portions of the island to see Etherington's former land and other sites associated with the 1779 invasion will most likely provide a memorable view. Experiencing that scenery along with the other breathtaking views of beautiful coastline, combined with this more recent reevalution of the 1781 Etherington/Morris Court-Martial Proceedings and the controversial surrender of St. Vincent's Island, perhaps one can truly sense the aura of the times and appreciate more fully the importance of these somewhat obscure events in this remote portion of the world.

View looking up the Leeward Coast from Fort Charlotte/Berkshire Hill where the Barracks were. The modern buildings at the bottom of the photo are Ottley Hall, unfortunately, a little used, 60 million dollar convention hall. Photo by: Co-author Rodger Durham.

Present day view (2001) of the interior of Fort Charlotte, built on Berkshire Hill and the former site of the Barracks used by the troops in 1779 as part of the defenses of Kingstown. The fort is maintained under the national auspices of St. Vincent and houses a museum of Carib history. Photo by: Co-author Rodger Durham.

♛ NOTES

[1]Captain Thomas Southey, *Chronological History of the West Indies*, In Three Volumes, (London, England: Frank Cass & Co., Ltd., 1827) Vol. II.

[2]Bryan Edwards, *History of...the West Indies*, (London: 2 Vols., 1793).

[3]Charles Shephard, Esquire, *An Historical Account of the Island of Saint Vincent*, (London: W. Nicol, Cleveland Row, St. James's, 1831); It should be noted that the Shephard account is an almost verbatim reprint of the Southey history listed above.

[4]Dr. Thomas Edward Coke, *A History of the West Indies, Containing the Natural, Civil and Ecclesiastical History of Each Island, with An Account of the Missions*, London, England, Three Volumes, 1810.

[5]Dr. Alexander Anderson (1748-1812), *Geography and History of St. Vincent's, West Indies*, Edited and Transcribed by Richard A. and Elizabeth S. Howard, (St. Vincent's, West Indies: Copy in the St. Vincent's Library, SVG 972.90 and No. 729844).

[6]Ivor Waters, *The Unfortunate Valentine Morris*, (Great Britain: The Chepstow Society, Chepstow, Mon., 1964).

[7]Dr. Todd E. Harburn, *The King's Quiet Commandant at Michilimackinac; A Biographical Sketch of Capt./Lt. Col. George Etherington of the 60th Royal American Regiment, Featuring His Heretofore Previously Unpublished Original Portrait, ca. 1787*, (Okemos, MI: The Michilimackinac Society Press, 4060 Leeward Drive, Publication No. 1, 1999).

[8]Waters, *op. cit.*; This book, a biography of Valentine Morris, essentially also relates the early history of St. Vincent's Island. It is largely based on Morris' own official governmental papers and correspondence as contained in both of the following: Valentine Morris, *A Narrative of the Official Conduct of Valentine Morris, Esq., Late Captain General, Governor in chief, & etc. & etc. Of the Island of St. Vincent's and its Dependencies*, (London, 1787); and *The Minutes of Council, Board of Trade and Secretary of State*, Public Record Office, [PRO] Colonial Office [C.O.], 26015, 1777.

9 What limited biographical information on Chatoyer that exists is contained in several sources which include the following: Sir William Young, *An Account of the Black Charibs in the Island of St. Vincent's*, (London: 1795, Printed for J. Sewell, Cornhill and Knight and Triphook, Booksellers to the King, St. Jame's Street, reprint edition Frank Cass & Co., London, 1971); Dr. I. Earl Kirby and C.I. Martin, *The Rise and Fall of the Black Caribs*, (St. Vincent's & The Grenadines National Trust, 1972); Shephard, *op. cit.*; Southey, *op. cit.*, Vols. I and II; and Dr. Alexander Anderson, *op. cit.*.

10 Fred Anderson, *Crucible of War, The Seven Years' War and the Fate of Empire in British North America, 1754-66*, (New York: Alfred A. Knopf/Random House, Inc., 2000), pp. 505-06. The Treaty of Paris was published in full in *The Gentleman's Magazine*, October 1763 (London, England: Printed by John Nichols, for David Henry, The Corner of St. Paul's Churchyard, Land gate), copy contained in the collections of the William L. Clements Library, University of Michigan, Ann Arbor, MI; it can also be found in Merrill Jense, Editor, "American Colonial Documents to 1776," *English Historical Documents*, (London, England, 1955), Vol. 9, pp. 640-43.

11 Lennox Honeychurch, *The Dominica Story*, (London and Oxford: Macmillan Education, Ltd., 1975), p. 47.

12 Andrew Jackson O'Shaughnessy, *An Empire Divided, The American Revolution and the British Caribbean*, (Philadelphia, PA: University of Pennsylvania Press, 2000), p. 41; also Waters, *op. cit.*, p. 30.

13 Shephard, *op. cit.*, p. 27.

14 Jan Rogozinski, *A Brief History of the Caribbean: From the Arawak and the Carib to the Present*, (New York, NY: Facts On File, Inc., 1992), p. 147.

15 *Ibid*, p. 78.

16 Shephard, *Ibid*, p. 26; Waters, *op. cit.*, p. 30; O'Shaughnessy, *op. cit.*, p. 41.

17 Rogozinski, *op. cit.*, p. 17.

[18] Honeychurch, *op. cit.*, pp. 11-19; also D.J.R. Walker, *Columbus and the Golden World of the Island Arawaks*, (Kingstown, Jamaica: Ian Randle Publishers, Ltd., 1992) pp. 24-28.

[19]Shephard, *op. cit.*, p. 1, Section 1.

[20]Rogozinski, *op. cit.*, p. 14.

[21]*Ibid*, p. 32.

[22]*Annual Register, (or a View of the History, Politics, and Literature) For the Year 1773*, (London, England: J. Dodsey, in Pall-Mall, 1773; The Internet Library of Early Journals, Joint Project of Birmingham, Manchester, Leeds, and Oxford Universities), Contents Section, p. 83; Southey, *op. cit.*, Vol. I, p. 259, Vol. II, p. 410; Waters, *op. cit.*, p. 30; Peter Hulme and Neil L. Whitehead, *Wild Majesty, Encounters with Caribs from Columbus to the Present Day, An Anthology*, (Oxford, Clarendon Press and the Oxford University Press, New York, 1992), p. 171; O'Shaughnessy, *op. cit.*, p. 41; Southey dates this incident as having occurred in 1674 and while his history lists the *Annual Register* as a source, the latter does not provide a specific date but rather suggests that this occurred in the late seventeenth century as does Waters, and O'Shaughnessy both of which followed much later. Interestingly, the Hulme/Whitehead book relates "The first mention of this event was in a deposition by Major John Scott, who dates it as 1635. "

[23]Sir William Young, *op. cit.*, p.

[24]O'Shaughnessy, *op. cit.*, p. 40.

[25]Rogozinski, *op. cit.*, p. 157; Young, *op. cit.*, p. 18.

[26]*Ibid.*

[27]O'Shaughnessy, *op. cit.*, p. 41; this is also mentioned in various other sources including surviving British military and civil government correspondence, too numerous to provide a comprehensive listing here. However, brief examples include: Dr. Alexander Anderson, *op. cit.*, discusses many of the "failings" of the British to deal realistically with the Caribs throughout his book; this is also suggested by Thomas Townsend, 1st Viscount Sydney, in two letters, Oct 1772, "Two points in opposition to the expedition against the Black Caribs on St. Vincent's," and Major

General William Dalrymple to Lord William Wildman Barrington, 2nd Viscount Barrington, St. Vincent's, October, 1772, both original letters contained in *The Sydney Papers*, in the collections of the William L. Clements Library, University of Michigan, Ann Arbor, MI; other sources include the aforementioned *Annual Register, 1773*, (Chronical Section for that year); and in a more recent book by Michael Craton, *Empire, Enslavement, and Freedom in the Caribbean*, (Kingston, Jamaica, Ian Randle Publishers, 1997, also same year by Markus Wiener Publishers, Princeton, N.J., USA, and James Currey Publishers, Oxford, England), Chapter 6, "Planter British Imperial Policy and the Black Caribs of St. Vincent's."

[28]Rogozinski, *op. cit.*, pp. 17, 152.

[29] Honeychurch, *op. cit.*, p. 62.

[30]Southey, *op. cit.*, Vol. II, p. 380; Shephard, *op. cit.*, p. 27.

[31]Southey, *Ibid.*

[32]*Ibid.*

[33]Young, pp. 19-20.

[34]Southey, *Ibid*; Waters, *op. cit.*, p. 30.

[35]Southey, *Ibid*, Vol. II, pp. 375, 378.

[36]Young, *op. cit.*, p. 20.

[37]*Fodor's Travel Guides, The Caribbean*, (New York, NY: Fodor's, Inc., 1986), p. 437; also John Macpherson, *Caribbean Lands, A Geography of the West Indies*, (London, England: Green & Co., Ltd., 1963, reprint ed., 1980, 1985), p. 110.

[38]Waters, *op. cit.*, p. 32.

[39]Frederick Bayley, *Four Years Residence in the West Indies, During the Years 1826-29, By The Son of a Military Man*, (London, 1831, Third Edition; William Kidd in Chandos St., West Strand, W.F. Wakeman, Dublin; Adam Black, Edinburgh and R. and J. Finlay, Glasgow, MDCCCXXXIII), p. 596; original book in personal collection of Mr. Felix

Dennis, Mustique, West Indies, previously on loan to co-author Mr. Durham.

[40]Young, *op. cit.*, pp. 20-21.

[41]*Ibid*, pp. 27-29.

[42] Edwards, *op. cit.*, Vol. II, pp. 318-322.

[43]*Ibid*, pp. 327-328.

[44]Fred Anderson, *Crucible of War, op. cit.*, pp. 641-691; O'Shaughnessy, *op. cit.*, pp. 81-108.

[45]O'Shaughnessy, *op. cit.*, pp. 82- 85.

[46]Craton, *op. cit.*, p. 120

[47] Southey, *op. cit.*, Vol. II, p. 381.

[48] Eric Williams, *From Columbus to Castro: The History of the Caribbean 1492-1969*, (New York, NY: Harper & Row, Publishers, 1970, Reprint ed. 1973), p. 187.

[49]Southey, *op. cit.*, Vol. II, p. 392-394.

[50]*Ibid*, p. 394; Williams, *Ibid*, p. 188.

[51]While too numerous to present an extensive list here of previous published articles and books on this topic, some of the more recent published books on Caribbean history with discussion and analysis of slave and maroon revolts include the following: Williams, *Ibid*, pp. 193-200; Rogozinski, *op. cit.*, pp. 152-161; Craton, *op. cit.*, and Craton, *Testing the Chains, Resistance to Slavery in the British West Indies*, (Ithaca, NY: Cornell University Press, 1982); O'Shaughnessy, *op. cit.*, pp. 34-48.

[52]Waters, *op. cit.*, p. 34.

[53]Young, *op. cit.*, p. 37.

[54]*Ibid*, pp. 49-50.

[55]*Annual Register, 1773, op. cit.*, p. 86; also Southey, *op. cit.*, Vol. II, p. 401-402.

[56]Ibid, p. 86, 89, Waters, *op. cit.*, p. 30; that the Caribs continued to be in correspondence with French officials in ensuing years is also noted in Southey, *Ibid*, Vol. II, p. 408.

[57]Young, *Ibid*, p. 61.

[58]*Ibid*, p. 64; *Annual Register, 1773*, p. 91.

[59]Southey, *op. cit.*, Vol. II, p. 408.

[60]Young, *op. cit.*, p. 75.

[61]*Annual Register, 1773, op. cit.*, Chronicle Section, pp. 89-90; also Southey, *op. cit.*, Vol. II, p. 414; Shephard, *op. cit.*, p. 35.

[62]*Sydney Papers (Papers of Thomas Townshend, 1st Viscount Sydney)*, "Strength of the Forces Employed at St. Vincent's" 1772 Dec. 24, according to the latest Returns, War Office; original in *Sydney Papers*, William L. Clements Library, University of Michigan, Ann Arbor, MI.

[63]*Annual Register, 1773, Ibid.*

[64]General Thomas Gage to Lord Viscount William Barrington, Secretary of War, 5 January 1773, New York; *The Correspondence of Thomas Gage*, Edited by Clarence Edwin Carter, (Yale Univeristy Press, 1933, reprint ed. Archon Books, Inc., 1969), Vol. II, p. 628; also O'Shaughnessy, *op. cit.*, p. 50; also *Sydney Papers*, 25 January 1773 – The State and Stations of His Majesty's Forces in St. Vincent's, as found in Bayley, *op. cit.*, pp. 126-127.

[65]*Annual Register, 1773, op. cit.*, Contents Section, p. 88; Southey, *op. cit.*, Vol. II, p. 410; Shephard, *op. cit.*, p. 29.

[66]Major General William Dalrymple to Lord William Barrington, 2nd Viscount Barrington, St. Vincent's, Oct. 1772, letter contained in *Sydney Papers, op. cit.*, Clements Library.

[67]*Ibid.*

[68]*Annual Register, 1773, Ibid*; Southey, *op. cit.*, Vol. II, p. 411.

[69]*Annual Register 1773, Ibid,* Chronicle Section, p. 89-90.

[70] *Annual Register, 1773, Ibid,* Chronicle Section, p. 104.

[71]*Ibid,* p. 247.

[72]Young, *op. cit.,* p. 97.

[73]Kirby and Martin, *op. cit.,* p. 25.

[74]O'Shaughnessy, *op. cit.,* p. 98.

[75] *Ibid,* p. 138; also Curtis P. Nettles, "The Founding Fathers and the West Indies: The Economics of Revolution," *The American Revolution and the West Indies,* Edited by Charles W. Toth, (Port Washington, NY/London, England: National University Publication, Kennikat Press, 1975), p. 68.

[76] Waters, *op. cit.,* p. 32.

[77]*Ibid,* p. 34.

[78]*Ibid,* pp. 39-44.

[79]Southey, *op. cit.,* Vol. II, p. 421.

[80]*Ibid,* p. 36; Shephard, *op. cit.,* p. 36.

[81] O'Shaughnessy, p. 213; 90% of gunpowder came from French ports in the Caribbean.

[82]*Ibid,* p. 155-157.

[83] Waters, *op. cit.,* p. 54.

[84]*Ibid,* p. 39.

[85]*Ibid,* p. 56.

[86]*Ibid,* p. 47; O'Shaughnessy, *op. cit.,* p. 53.

[87]O'Shaughnessy, *Ibid*, p. 51.

[88]*Ibid*, pp. 47-56.

[89]*Ibid*, pp. 38, 52-53.

[90]Waters, *op. cit.*, 42-47.

[91]O'Shaughnessy, *op. cit.*, p. 49.

[92] Waters, *op. cit.*, pp. 45-46.

[93]*Ibid*, p. 62, also pp. 45-46; O'Shaughnessy, *op. cit.*, pp. 169-170.

[94]Waters, *Ibid*, p. 39.

[95]Southey, *op. cit.*, Vol. II, p. 425.

[96]Waters, *op. cit.*, p. 58; see also Note 128.

[97]*Ibid*, p. 44; also from Minutes of Council, Board of Trade and Secretary of State, PRO, Colonial Office [CO], 260/4, 1777.

[98]Letter of Captain Robert Morse, Commanding Engineers in the Ceded Islands including St. Vincent's to Lord William Barrington, 26 May 1777 at Grenada; and reply letter of Barrington to Morse 11 August 1777 (Morse was then at St. Vincent's), both original letters in the *National Archives of Scotland*, Reference GD 46/17/1, C 36110; copies in personal collections of the co-authors.

[99]William Seymour, *The Price of Folly, British Blunders in the War of American Independence*, (London, England, and Washington, D.C., USA: Brassey's Ltd, and Inc., 1995), p. 129.

[100]Waters, *op. cit.*, pp. 49-50.

[101]*Ibid*, p. 61.

[102]O'Shaughnessy, *op. cit.*, p. 117.

[103]Southey, *op. cit.*, Vol. II, p. 442; Shephard, *op. cit.*, p. 39.

[104]*Ibid.*

[105]Waters, *op. cit.*, p. 45.

[106]Southey, *op. cit.*, Vol. II, p. 441; Shephard, *op. cit.*, p. 39.

[107]Waters, *op. cit.*, p. 66.

[108]Southey, *op. cit.*, Vol. II, p. 442; Shephard, *op. cit.*, p. 40; Waters, *Ibid.*

[109]*Ibid.*

[110]Waters, *op. cit.*, p. 71.

[111]Waters, *Ibid*, p. 45; also *St. Vincent's Handbook, Directory, & Almanac for the Year 1914*, Editor Robert M. Anderson, (Colony of St. Vincent's, West Indies: "Conferred on the Colony by Her Highness, Princess Maria Louisa of Schleswig Holstein as a result of her one month's stay"), original is in the personal collection of Sir James, former Prime Minister of St. Vincent's. Transcribed excerpts in the personal collection of co-author Mr. Durham.

[112]The first names of the 60th officers and non-commissioned officers (NCO's) involved in the 1779 St. Vincent's events were not mentioned in the previous written histories or the trial transcript itself. These, however, were found in the *British Army List For the Year 1779* (i.e. *A List of the General and Field Officers as They Rank in The Army...with the Dates of Their Commissions)*, and the *Muster Rolls of the 60th Regiment*, War Office files, WO 12/6935 respectively, both in the Public Record Office, Kew, Richmond, Surrey, England. Those noted in the Witness List, testimony, and/or description of events as found in the aforementioned documents are as follows: Capt. William Kelly, Lt. David Gordon, Lt. Thomas Barker, Lt. Thomas Walker and Ensign Hubert [Van] Hamell (the latter was promoted to Lieutenant on 15 Aug 1781 according to the *1783 British Army List*) while the NCO's were Sgt. John Ayers and Sgt. John McMullin [McMullen or McMullan]; according to the *Dec 1779-Feb 1780 List*, Ayers was still a Sgt. at that date.

[113]Waters, *Ibid*, p. 70.

[114]The entire Etherington Court-martial original transcript is in the collections of the Public Record Office/War Office files, Kew, Richmond,

Surrey, England; PRO/WO 71/58, pp. 271-337, copy in personal collections of co-authors, initially obtained by co-author Dr. Harburn.

[115]Sir William Young, *op. cit.*, p. 101.

[116]Dr. Alexander Anderson, *op. cit.*

[117] Shephard, *op. cit.*, p. 43-44.

[118]Southey, *op. cit.*, Vol. II, p. 443-44. Here, Southey's history contains a complete copy of the *Articles of Capitulation...over His Majesty's Island of St. Vincent's and its dependencies...*, (the terms were originally published in *The St. Vincent's Gazette 1779*) which as noted, are essentially the same terms granted the British at Dominica eight months prior. (Note: The Capitulation is comprised of thirty-six articles, although only those having direct relevance to the charges in the trial have been presented for discussion in the Epilogue here.)

[119]*Ibid*, p. 446.

[120]Waters, *op. cit.*, p. 68.

[121]*Ibid*, p. 69.

[122]Brian Leigh Dunnigan, *Siege-1759, The Campaign Against Niagara*, (Youngstown, NY: Old Fort Niagara Association, Inc., Revised Ed., 1996), pp. 5-7, 128; see also Sebastien Le Prestre de Vauban, *A Manual of Siegecraft and Fortification*, (Ann Arbor, MI: University of Michigan Press, 1968, translated from 1740).

[123]Shephard, *op. cit.*, p. 43; also Dr. Thomas Coke, *A History of the West Indies*, (London: 1810), p. 195.

[124]*Ibid*; Waters, *op. cit.*, p. 66.

[125]Waters, *Ibid*, p. 45.

[126]Dr. David A. Armour and Dr. Keith R. Widder, *At the Crossroads, Michilimackinac During the American Revolution*, (Mackinac Island, MI: Mackinac State Historic Parks/Mackinac Island State Park Commission, 1978), p. 119. Another example of the dichotomy between civil and military authority is demonstrated by the situation at Michilimackinac in

the Upper Great Lakes in North America during the American Revolution. Captain Patrick Sinclair, Commandant of Fort Michilimackinac (and Fort Mackinac which he designed and built to replace the latter) was commissioned as Lieutenant Governor and Superintendent of Michilimackinac and its dependencies in April 1775, holding that position until September 1782. Initially, as Governor, his administrative authority was restricted to civil responsibilities only. He did not, however, have auspices over the garrison troops there until receiving a commission as Captain in the 84th or Royal Highland Emigrant Regiment of Foot. Prior to then, this caused many problems between soldiers, traders, and other inhabitants of the community over disputes involving civil law and military matters as the troops were under the command of the senior most regular officer of the garrison.

[127]O'Shaughnessy, *op. cit.*, p. 55.

[128]Waters, *op. cit.*, p. 57; also *Shelburne Papers*, (The Papers of Lord William Petty Shelburne, Earl of Shelburne, British Secretary of State 1782-83), originals in Clements Library, University of Michigan, Vol. 78, 353, 359, 363, and 374, July 22, 1778 Declarations of Dr. John Connor, Duncan Campbell, LK Phipps, and Levi Porter respectively to Henry Sharpe, Esq., President of His Majesty's Council and Chief Justice of His Majesty's Court of Common Pleas at St. Vincent's Island. These declarations, made under oath to Sharpe (who was at odds with the Governor and whose brother was married to Morris's niece as previously mentioned), also point out the questionable practices of Governor Morris in making land grants/rents at St. Vincent's including those to his sister Caroline who resided in England. In particular, Dr. Connor's declaration accuses the Governor of intentionally reneging on a land grant of 19 acres that Connor had made in agreement to purchase from Marie Letrain, a free Negro woman on the island, a transaction that had been personally signed and approved by Morris and that he falsely pretended to be ignorant of while proceeding to officially grant the land to his sister. Ironically, Connor and Campbell were Prosecution Witnesses for Morris at the Court-martial and Porter was a Surveyor for the Governor in 1778 during some of these land transactions.

[129]*Ibid*, p. 40.

[130]"The Memorial of Lieutenant Colonel George Etherington of his Majesty's Sixtieth Regiment of Foot stationed in the Island of Saint Vincent in the West Indies" to the Lords Commissioners of his Majesty's

Treasury, 17 January 1776: Treasury Chambers, PRO, T1/521, 247-249, copy in personal collection of Dr. Harburn.

[131]Waters, *op. cit.*, p. 68; Shephard, *op. cit.*, p. 38.

[132]General Thomas Gage (1719-1787), born in Sussex, England, was a career army officer and veteran of the French and Indian War. He had been Commander-in-Chief of British Forces in America from November 1763 through the beginning of the American Revolution in April 1775 at Lexington and Concord in Massachusetts until being relieved of those duites in September later that year. His seemingly apparent animosity toward Etherington may have resulted from a prior incident involving Etherington back in 1772 while the latter (then a Major in rank) was Commandant at Fort Niagara in New York. A renegade English trader named David Ramsay had been accused by Missisaga Indians in upper western New York of murdering eight of their tribe including two women and a child between March and April of 1772. Ramsay, in a declaration to Etherington, claimed the alleged murders were in self-defense from attacks by the intoxicated Indians over a dispute concerning rum and trade goods. The Indians subsequently complained to Sir William Johnson, the well-known and powerful British Superintendent of Indian Affairs in North America, who in turn informed Gage. Gage criticized Etherington's handling of the incident in essence insinuating that the Major had been naive and duped by Ramsay in allowing him (along with another potential witness to the incident) to go free. In an effort to keep peace, the Indians were provided an apology and gifts, while Ramsay was later brought to trial in Montreal, Canada by order of Gage and Johnson.

While Ramsay admitted to the killings and was likely most responsible for the quarrel, it is very apparent that the Indians, on the other hand, were also not entirely innocent and just as disingenuous in not relating the truth about the affair. Etherington, it would appear, simply noted the incident while initially accepting Ramsay's declaration at the time since no other opposing evidence was readily available. As a result, although it is speculation, he may have perhaps done so to allow Johnson to eventually handle the affair. Yet, some criticism is not without warrant as the more proper course would have been to detain Ramsay until further corroborating or refuting evidence could be obtained.

Nonetheless, in reviewing the surviving original correspondence concerning this unfortunate incident, which eventually became referred to as the Ramsay/Etherington Incident, it is obvious that Gage (and Johnson as well) was quite prejudicial in siding entirely with the Indians and condemning Ramsay as guilty even before the trial, thereby violating the well-known accepted premise of "innocent until proven guilty." It appears that Gage had already determined his opinion on the matter from the beginning, based on initially hearing only one side of the story i.e. that of his longtime friend and colleague Johnson (even during the French and Indian War years, Gage is known to have had a propensity for considering only one side or alternative in making judgements without having all relevant facts and/or promoting his own personal agendas). As such, it is not unreasonable to suggest (in essence it is rather evident from his own remarks about Etherington's "lack of zeal") that Gage had a previously established dislike for Etherington thereby easily recommending years later that the former St. Vincent's commander stand trial before a Court-martial in 1781 to face Morris's charges.

This incident provides an interesting (and relevant) sidelight to the later Etherington/Morris dispute. The sequence of events concerning the above is contained in several letters of *The Papers of Sir William Johnson*, Edited by Dr. Alexander C. Flick (Albany, NY: The University of the State of New York [SUNY], 1933), Vol. VIII, *Declaration of David Ramsay to George Etherington, May 15, 1772*, pp. 482-86, *Johnson to Gage, May 27, 1772*, pp. 495-97, *Johnson to Etherington, June 7, 1772*, pp. 512-15, *Gage to Johnson, Sept, 7, 1772*, pp. 592-94; also Vol. XII, Edited by Dr. Albert B. Corey, (Albany, NY: SUNY, 1957), *Johnson's Speech of Missisagas, May 26, 1772*, p. 963, *Gage to Johnson, June 3, 1772*, p. 964, and *Gage to Johnson, November 30, 1772*, p. 1005.

[133]Shephard, *op. cit.*, p. 44; Waters, *op. cit.*, p.71.

[134]Valentine Morris to Lord William Petty Shelburne, Earl of Shelburne, 10 February 1783, *Shelburne Papers, op. cit.*, Vol. 78, 63; and also Morris to Lord Shelburne, 29 March 1780, *Shelburne Papers*, Vol. 78, 345.

[135]O'Shaughnessy, *op. cit.*, p. 210.

[136]Southey, *op. cit.*, Vol. II, p. 475.

[137]*Ibid*, p. 479.

[138] Lowell J. Ragatz, "The Sugar Colonies During the Revolution," *The American Revolution and the West Indies*, Edited by Charles W. Toth, *op. cit.*, p. 83.

[139]Southey, *op. cit.*, p. 542.

[140]*British Army Lists, i.e. A List of the General and Field Officers as They Rank in The Army,...with the Dates of Their Commissions* (London, England: Public Record Office [PRO], 1783; hereafter cited as *British Army Lists*; also copy contained in the National Archives of Canada [NAC].

[141]Co-author Dr. Harburn's personal communication, letter of 9 November 1996, with Colonel (Retd) I.H. McCausland, then Director (Curator), The Royal Green Jackets Museum, Regimental Headquarters, Peninsula Barracks, Romsey Road, Winchester, Hants, England SO23 8TS.

[142] Herbert Fairlie Wood, *The King's Royal Rifle Corps*, Edited by Lt. General Sir Brian Horrocks, (London, England: Harrish Hamilton, Ebenezer Baylis and Son, Ltd., The Trinity Press, 1967), p. 29.

[143]Harburn, *King's Quiet Commandant...Etherington, op. cit.*, p. 19.

[144]*Ibid*; Public Record Office/War Office files; PRO/WO 12/6871 Muster Rolls 60th Regiment, January 1788 to December 1788, this important and previously unknown information was located for and first published by Dr. Harburn in the Etherington biographical vignette.

[145]Harburn, *Ibid*; personal communication with Colonel McCausland, *op. cit.*

[146]Waters, *op. cit.*, p. 74.

[147]*Data Wales, Index-Search*, (www.data-wales.co.uk) Internet Web site for information concerning historical sites, museums, societies and related topics in the area of Chepstow in Monmouthshire, south Wales, U.K.

[148]Young, *op. cit.*, pp. 107-108; Southey, *op. cit.*, Vol. III, p. 83.

[149]Shephard, *op. cit.*, pp. 73-74; Southey, *Ibid.*

[150]Virginia Radcliff, *The Caribbean Heritage*, (New York, NY: Walker and Co., 1976), p. 38.

✾ APPENDIX 1

"Strength of the Forces employed at St. Vincents, 1772 Dec. 24"

Strength of the undermentioned Regiments & Detachments according to the latest Returns

	Sergeants	Drums	Effective Rank & File
6 Regt. & Embarkation Return the 10 Oct	20	12	351
14th & Return 10 September	19	11	330
31st & Embarkation Return 12 August	14	8	301
32nd & Return 1st October	20	12	212
60th & Return 1st August	19	11	332
70th Detachment & Return 1st October	3	2	62
			1596

War office 24 Decr 1772

Original Return from the *Sydney Papers*, Thomas Townsend, 1st Viscount Sydney, 24 December 1772, in collections of the William L. Clements Library, University of Michigan. Cited and used with permission, Courtesy: William L. Clements Library, University of Michigan.

⚜ APPENDIX 2

ARTICLES OF CAPITULATION AT THE ISLAND OF ST. VINCENT'S, JUNE 18,1779

*Originally published in the *St. Vincent Gazette, 1779*; again in Dr. Thomas Edward Coke's *A History of the West Indies*, (London, England, 1810), Vol. II, p. 195; and later in Captain Thomas Southey's *Chronological History of the West Indies in Three Volumes*, (London, England, 1827, reprint edition 1968), Vol. II, pp. 443-45.

Articles of Capitulation between Le Chevalier de Trolong du Rumain, Lieutenant of His most Christian Majesty, Commander-in-Chief of the French Troops, and his Excellency Valentine Morris, Esquire, Captain-General and Governor-in-Chief in and over His Majesty's Island of St. Vincent and its dependencies, Chancellor, Ordinary, and Vice-Admiral of the same, &c. &c.

"**ARTICLE 1.** Governor Morris demands in the first place, that the officer and drummer sent by him yesterday to the commander of the French troops be restored to him; the detaining these when sent as a flag of truce, and then continuing to march on, appearing to him to have been a great infringement of the laws of war.

"**ANSWER.** Granted.

"**2.** The governor and staff officers, soldiers and artillerymen, to be carried to the island of Antigua, in good vessels, sufficiently victualled at the expence of His most Christian Majesty, and there to be at liberty to do duty. The governor engaging an equal number of equal qualities of French prisoners to be exchanged in their room, the same for one officer of engineers and an assistant engineer.

"**ANSW.** The troops shall be exchanged at Antigua for an equal number of French prisoners.

"**4.** The officers and others shall have liberty to carry their wives and families and domestic slaves to the English islands by the shortest route, and that they shall be furnished with good vessels and provisions for the passage.

"**ANSW.** Granted.

"**5.** The inhabitants of the island shall march out of their posts with the honours of war, their baggage, arms, and colours, drums beating, and lighted matches.

"**ANSW.** The inhabitants shall go freely to their homes.

"**6.** The inhabitants of the island shall continue to enjoy their civil government, their laws, usages, and ordinances. Justice shall be administered by the same persons that are now in office, and the interior police of the island shall be settled between His most Christian Majesty's governor and the inhabitants; and in case the island be ceded to the King of France at the peace, the inhabitants shall be at liberty either to preserve their political government, or to accept that which is established in Martinico and the French islands.

"**ANSW.** Granted.

"**7.** The inhabitants, both secular and clergy, shall be maintained in the possession of their real and personal estates and property, of what nature soever, as well as in the enjoyment of their rights and privileges, honours and immunities, and the free Negroes and Mulattoes in their freedom.

"**ANSW.** Granted.
"**8.** That they shall pay no other duty to His most Christian Majesty than they paid to His Britannic Majesty, without any other tax or impost; the expence of the administration of justice, the salaries of ministers, and other ordinary charges, shall be paid out of the revenues of His most Christian Majesty, in like manner as under the government of His Britannic Majesty.

"**ANSW.** Granted if it was granted at Dominica.

"**9.** That the slaves, baggage, vessels, merchandise, and every thing else taken since the landing of the French troops, and during the attack of the island, shall be restored.

"ANSW. Granted as far as it possibly can be effected.

"10. THE ABSENT INHABITANTS, AND THOSE IN THE SERVICE OF His Britannic Majesty, shall be maintained in the enjoyment and possession of their estates and effects, which shall be managed by their attornies.

"ANSW. Granted.

"11. The inhabitants shall not be compelled to furnish quarters or any thing else for the troops, or slaves to work on the fortifications.

"ANSW. This article cannot be granted.

"12. The ships, vessels, and droghers belonging to the inhabitants of this island, shall remain their property.

"ANSW. Granted.

"13. The widows and other inhabitants, who from sickness or other obstacles cannot sign the capitulation, shall have a limited time to agree to it.

"ANSW. Granted.

"14. The inhabitants and merchants of the island comprehended in the present capitulation, shall enjoy all the privileges of trade on the same terms as are granted to the subjects of His most Christian Majesty throughout the extent of his dominions.

"ANSW. Granted.

"15. The inhabitants shall observe a strict neutrality, and not be forced to take up arms against His Britannic Majesty, or any other power.

"ANSW. Granted.

"16. The inhabitants shall enjoy the free exercise of their religion and the ministers their curacies.

"ANSW. Granted.

"17. All the prisoners taken or persons detained since the landing of the French troops shall be reciprocally restored.

"ANSW. Granted.

"18. Merchants of the island may receive ships to their address without being confiscated, dispose of their merchandise, and carry on trade; and the port shall be entirely free on paying the same duties as in the French islands.
"ANSW. Agreed, provided they wear French colours after they arrive.

"19. The inhabitants shall keep their arms.

"ANSW. Rejected.

"20. No persons but those now resident on the island, or at present proprietors of lands and houses, shall hold any house or land by purchase, or otherwise, until the peace; but at the peace, if this island be ceded to the King of France, the inhabitants who decline living under the French government, may then be at liberty to sell their estates, both real and personal, to whom they please, and to retire whenever they shall think proper, for which purpose a reasonable time shall be allowed.

"ANSW. Granted.

"21. The inhabitants of the island may send their children to be educated in England, as well as to send them back, and to make remittances for their maintenance while in England.

"ANSW. Granted.

"22. The inhabitants shall be at liberty to sell their estates and effects to whom they may think fit.

"ANSW. Granted.

"23. That the court of chancery shall be held by the members of the council, and the proceedings be the same as are now used in the island of Antigua except that all writs and other process shall be granted by the president of the council; and the great seal now used in the island shall be given into and remain in his custody for the purpose of sealing all writs, process, and decrees issuing out and made by the said court.

"ANSW. Granted if it was granted to Dominica.

"24. That the wives of such officers and others as are not in the island may retire with their effects, and the number of domesties, according to their rank.

"ANSW. Granted.

"25. There shall be delivered to the general of the French troops all the artillery and sotes in the colony of St. Vincent's belonging to the King of England. All the batteries on the coast, and the respective posts, as well in the Carib country or elsewhere in the island, shall be surrendered in the same state they were in when the island was attacked, such injury as these may have received in any attack excepted. All the arms belonging to the King of England's troops shall be delivered in like condition, excepting those of the officers of the troops and militia. No powder shall be secreted or carried out of the magazines, which shall be delivered by the governor.

"ANSW. Granted.

"26. None of the Indians or Caribs shall on any account be permitted to garrison or be quartered in any of the forts, posts, towns, or houses in the island, and the inhabitants demand and expect the protection of His most Christian Majesty's commander to preserve their persons and properties inviolate, so long as they faithfully observe the present articles of capitulation.

"ANSW. Granted with the exception in the reference.

"27. All Negroes now absent or runaway, shall, when taken and brought in, be delivered to their proprietors; and if any such are harboured by the Indians, Caribs, or free Negroes, they shall, upon demand, be restored.

"ANSW. Granted.

"28. Whatever depredations the Caribs have committed during or since the attack of the island, they to be compelled to instantly desist therefrom, and be made to release and give up all slaves and effects which they have taken, and to be fully restrained from hereafter committing the least disorders on the persons and effects of the inhabitants.

"**ANSW.** As much justice as possible shall be rendered.

"**29.** All the Caribs now under arms, and who have joined the French troops, to be immediately disarmed, dismissed, and ordered to their respective homes; and all others now in arms to be disarmed, and also compelled to retire to their respective homes, and to remain in their own districts.

"**ANSW.** Granted, with the exception in the reference.

"**30.** A safeguard to be granted for all the papers at the government-house, and these not to be liable to any inspection; and Governor Morris to be at liberty either to keep those there or to remove them.

"**ANSW.** Granted.

"**31.** The like to be granted for all papers and records in the respective offices of the customs, the marshal, secretary, and register, receiver-general, treasurer, and commissary, and of all other public records and papers, to be left in the custody of their respective officers, and not to be inspected.

"**ANSW.** Granted.

"**32.** Permission to send either to England, or to some of his Majesty's admirals or governors, advice, to be forwarded to His Britannic Majesty of the present event.

"**ANSW.** Whenever the governor thinks proper.

"**33.** Governor Morris to remain in the island some time in order to settle his own private affairs, as also any of the King's officers, if required.
"**ANSW.** Granted.

Articles demanded by the French General.

"ARTICLE 34. The inhabitants shall not be obliged to pay any debts due to English persons not residing in this island, and who are not capitulants thereof, until the end of the war.

"35. All vessels taken after the capitulation will be restored.

"ANSW. Granted, with the exception in the reference.

"36. The colony shall be obliged to advance a sum of money to pay the French troops, which shall be discounted from the revenue.

"We, the commander-in-chief of the French troops, legally authorized in the King's name by the Count d'Estaing and Valentine Morris, Esquire, governor-in-chief of the island of St. Vincent, have agreed to and signed three copies of the above thirty-six articles.

"Le Chev. de Trolong du Rumain.
"Par ordre, Dallan, Secretaire.
"Valentine Morris.
"By command, R. Westfield, Sec.
"Government-House, St. Vincent's,
        "June 18th, 1779."

References.

"1. As to the 29th article, although Mr. Canonge had allowed it, if it has been agreed that the Caribs shall be sent to their homes, and there be restrained from doing injury to the inhabitants and red Caribs, without disarming them.

"2. Relative to the 26th article, after the words 'in any of the forts,' there shall be understood, 'except in case of an attack.'

"3. The ships from Europe made an exception to the 35th article.

"Le Chev. de Trolong du Rumain.
"Par ordre, Dallan, Secretaire.
"Valentine Morris.
"R. Westfield, Secretary.

⚜ BIBLIOGRAPHY

As previously noted in the preface, the list of books, articles, and essays relating the military, cultural and socioeconomic history of the West Indies (inclusive of both published and unpublished materials as well as those currently out of print) is enormous, so much that it is not possible due to space limitations, nor reasonable to list them all here. As renowned Caribbean historian Dr. Michael Craton has aptly noted many "are hidden away in a variety of journals, conference proceedings, festschrifts, multi-authored commissioned collections, and encyclopedias" and similar endeavors making it difficult for many readers to obtain access to them. Interested readers who desire more in-depth study of Caribbean history are recommended to consult the bibliography sections of some of the more recently published books regarding these various topics which contain extensive reference listings.

Nonetheless, the following select bibliography is listed containing the significant sources utilized and consulted for purposes of this book and which should provide the reader with an adequate and representative listing of resources. The designation between primary and secondary source material is obvious (including distinction between published books and original manuscript collections) and these references have been combined here which is most efficient rather than being listed as separate sections.

Anderson, Dr. Alexander (1748-1812), *Geography and History of St. Vincent, West Indies*, Edited by, Richard A. and Elizabeth S. Howard, St. Vincent Library, St. Vincent, West Indies.

Anderson, Fred, *Crucible of War, The Seven Years' War and the Fate of Empire in British North America, 1754-66*, New York, New York, Alfred A. Knopf/Random House, Inc., 2000.

Anderson, Robert M., Editor, *St. Vincent's Handbook, Directory & Almanac for the Year 1914*, St. Vincent's, West Indies, original in a private collection in the West Indies.

Annual Register, (or a View of History, Politics, and Literature) For the Year 1773, London, England, J. Dodsey, in Pall-Mall, 1773, available per The Internet Library of Early Journals, Joint Project of Birmingham, Manchester, Leeds, and Oxford Universities.

Bayley, Frederick, *Four Years Residence in the West Indies, During the Years 1826-29, By The Son of a Military Man*, London, England, 1831, original in a private collection in Mustique, West Indies.

British Army Lists, i.e. A List of the General and Field Officers as They Rank in The Army...with the Dates of Their Commissions, London, Public Record Office (PRO), copies also contained in the William L. Clements Library, University of Michigan, Ann Arbor, Michigan, and the National Archives of Canada, Ottawa, Ontario, Canada.

Carter, Clarence E., Editor, *The Correspondence of Thomas Gage*, Yale University Press, 1933, Reprint Edition, Archon Books, Inc., 1969.

Coke, Dr. Thomas Edward, *A History of the West Indies, Containing the Natural, Civil and Ecclesiastical History of Each Island, with An Account of the Missions*, London, England, Three Volumes, 1810.

Craton, Michael, *Testing the Chains, Resistance to Slavery in the British West Indies*, Ithaca, New York, Cornell University Press, 1982.

_____, *Empire, Enslavement, and Freedom in the Caribbean*, Kingstown, Jamaica, Ian Randle Publishers, and Princeton, New Jersey, Markus Wiener Publishers, 1997.

Edwards, Bryan, *History of...the West Indies*, London, England, Two Volumes, 1793.

Gage Papers (The Papers of General Thomas Gage), American Series, originals in the William L. Clements Library, University of Michigan, Ann Arbor, Michigan.

Gentlemen's Magazine, (and Historical Chronicle), London, England, Printed by John Nichols, for David Henry, Corner of St. Paul's Churchyard, 1739-1789, copies in the William L. Clements Library.

Germain Papers (The Papers of Lord George Germain, Secretary of State 1775-1782), originals in William L. Clements Library.

Harburn, Dr. Todd E., *The King's Quiet Commandant at Michilimackinac; A Biographical Sketch of Capt./Lt. Col. George Etherington of the 60th Royal American Regiment, Featuring His Heretofore Previously Unpublished Original Portrait ca. 1787*, Okemos, Michigan, The Michilimackinac Society Press, Publication No.1, 1999.

Honeychurch, Lennox, *The Dominica Story*, London and Oxford, England, Macmillan Education, Ltd., 1975.

Hulme, Peter, and Whitehead, Neil L., *Wild Majesty, Encounters with Caribs from Columbus to the Present Day, An Anthology*, Oxford, England, Oxford and New York, Oxford University Press and Clarendon Press, 1992.

Kirby, Dr. I. Earl and Martin, C.I., *The Rise and Fall of the Black Caribs*, St. Vincent & The Grenadines National Trust, West Indies, 1972.

Morris, Valentine, Esq., *A Narrative of the Official Conduct of Valentine Morris, Esq., Late Captain and General, Governor in Chief, & etc. & etc. Of the Island of St. Vincent and its Dependencies*, London, England, British Library, 1787.

National Archives of Scotland, military correspondence 1773-77 of Lord Viscount William Barrington, British Secretary of War.

O'Shaughnessy, Andrew Jackson, *An Empire Divided, The American Revolution and the British Caribbean*, Philadelphia, Pennsylvania, University of Pennsylvania Press, 2000.

Public Record Office, Kew, Richmond, Surrey, England (PRO), War Office Papers (WO) 71/58, *The Proceedings of a General Court Martial held on the Island of St. Lucia, West Indies, The Fifth Day of October 1781; Valentine Morris, Esq., late Governor of the Island of St. Vincent against Lt. Colonel George Etherington, of the 2nd Battalion, 60th or Royal American Regiment*, original Etherington Court Martial transcripts.

_____, Colonial Office Papers (CO) 260, 263, St. Vincent, *The Minutes of Council, Board of Trade and Secretary of State.*

_____, Treasury Chambers, T1/521, 247-249, "The Memorial of Lieutenant Colonel George Etherington of His Majesty's Sixtieth Regiment of Foot Stationed in the Island of Saint Vincent in the West Indies," to the Lords Commissioners of His Majesty's Treasury

Radcliff, Virginia, *The Caribbean Heritage*, New York, New York, Walker and Co., 1976.

Ragatz, Lowell J., *The Fall of the Planter Class in the British West Indies, 1763-1833*, New York, 1928.

Rogozinski, Jan, *A Brief History of the Caribbean; From the Arawak and the Carib to the Present*, New York, New York, Facts on File, Inc., 1992.

Seymour, William, *The Price of Folly, British Blunders in the War of American Independence*, London, England, and Washington, D.C., Brassey's, Ltd., and Inc., 1995.

Shephard, Charles, *An Historical Account of the Island of Saint Vincent*, London, England, W. Nicol, Cleveland Row, St. James's, 1831.

Shelburne Papers (The Papers of Lord William Petty, Earl of Shelburne, Secretary of State 1782-83), originals in William L. Clements Library.

Southey, Captain Thomas, *Chronological History of the West Indies, In Three Volumes*, London, England, 1827, Reprint Edition, Frank Cass & Co., Ltd, 1968.

Sydney Papers (The Papers of Townsend, Thomas, (1732-1800), 1st Viscount Sydney), originals in the collections of the William L. Clements Library, University of Michigan, Ann Arbor, Michigan.

Toth, Charles, W., Editor, *The American Revolution and the West Indies*, Port Washington, New York/London, England, National University Publication, Kennikat Press, 1975.

Waters, Ivor, *The Unfortunate Valentine Morris*, The Chepstow Society, Chepstow, Great Britain, 1964.

Williams, Eric, *From Columbus to Castro: The History of the Caribbean 1492-1969*, New York, New York, Harper & Row, Publishers, 1970, Reprint Edition, 1973.

Wood, Herbert Fairlie, *The King's Royal Rifle Corps*, Edited by Lt. General Sir Brian Horrocks, London, England, Harrish Hamilton, Ebenezer Baylis and Son, Ltd., The Trinity Press, 1967.

Young, Sir William (The Son), *An Account of the Black Charibs in the Island of St. Vincent's*, London, England, 1795, Reprint Edition Frank Cass & Co., London, 1971.

⚜ INDEX

Dr. Todd E. Harburn

Rodger Durham

⌘ ABOUT THE AUTHORS

Dr. Todd Harburn is a man of many talents and interests.

A native of Flint, Michigan, Todd attended Hope College, where he majored in pre-med and earned all conference honors in football.

After graduating from the Chicago College of Osteopathic Medicine, he completed an orthopedic surgery residency, and in addition to his orthopedic surgery/sportsmedicine practice, he is a football team physician for Alma College.

Todd has had a nearly lifelong interest in the British 60th or Royal American Regiment and its related history to the French and Indian War, Pontiac's Conspiracy, and the American Revolution.

Having done extensive research on several of the officers and garrisons of the 60th Regiment in the Great Lakes region, he has had several publications on these topics in recent years.

His first book, *Of Scarlet and Blue: The 60th Royal American Regimental Coat 1755-1768* (with R. Scott Stephenson), set the standard for the uniform coats used by most British French and Indian War reenactors today, and was the basis for the pattern for the British uniforms in the movie, *The Last of the Mohicans* (1991).

He was also a consultant, assisted in research, wrote a portion of the script for two episodes, assisted in coordinating filming of several scenes, and portrayed General Jeffery Amherst and Captain George Etherington in the A&E/History Channel's 1997 award winning *Frontier: Legends of the Old Northwest*.

A reenactor as well, he has portrayed Etherington for several years in the Annual Fort Michilimackinac Pageant at the reconstructed fort in upper Michigan.

Todd also has other areas of historical interest including the Alamo and college football. He contributed an essay on the controversial death of David Crockett in the *Alamo Sourcebook 1836: A Comprehensive Guide to the Alamo and the Texas Revolution*, by Tim and Terry Todish (1998, Eakin Press) and has also co-authored two college football history books: *MIAA FOOTBALL: The Illustrated Gridiron History of the Michigan Intercollegiate Athletic Association* (with his father Gerald E. Harburn), and *Alma College Football: A Centennial Salute to the Champions, 100 Years of Alma College Football 1894-1994* (with Dr. Charles A. Gray).

Todd currently resides in Okemos, Michigan, with wife Shirley, and daughters Shannon and Stacey.

♔   ♔   ♔

Born of Canadian parents in Kenmore, New York, Rodger Durham attended New York University earning a B.A. in Geology; this was followed up by graduate work at U.C.L.A. in Petroleum Engineering.

Owing to a depressed oil business, he changed venues to the plastics industry, and while climbing the management chairs, obtained an M.B.A. (and three children). After several years, while residing in Texas, Rodger founded his own engineered-plastics company. After enjoying quite a successful run over the years, he was able to retire and realize two life-long goals: building a home on a tropical island (Bequia Island, St. Vincent & the Grenadines, West Indies) and being able to indulge his passion for pre-nineteenth century history of the area.

With regard to the latter, for the past five years, Rodger has worked on his "hobby" (when not playing tennis, sailing or fishing), and has compiled a data-base of over 2,200 pages.